George
Washington

'oung Leader

Illustrated by E. Joseph Dreany

George Washington

Young Leader

By Augusta Stevenson

THE BOBBS-MERRILL COMPANY, INC.
INDIANAPOLIS/NEW YORK

PUBLISHED BY THE BOBBS-MERRILL CO., INC.
INDIANAPOLIS/NEW YORK

MANUFACTURED IN THE UNITED STATES OF AMERICA

Library of Congress Cataloging in Publication Data
Stevenson, Augusta.
George Washington, young leader.

Originally published as: George Washington, boy leader.
1959.
Summary: Presents the boyhood of the Revolutionary leader
and first President of the United States.
1. Washington, George, 1732–1799—Childhood and youth—
Juvenile literature. 2. Presidents—United States—Biography—
Juvenile literature. [1. Washington, George, 1732–1799. 2.
Presidents] I. Title.
E312.2.S83 1984 973.4'1'0924 [B] [92] 83-15691
ISBN 0-672-52801-0 (pbk.)

*Dedicated to the
memory of a fine patriot,
my mother,
Polly Ann Van Houten Stevenson*

Illustrations

Full pages

Numerous smaller illustrations

Contents

Books by Augusta Stevenson

ABRAHAM LINCOLN:
THE GREAT EMANCIPATOR

ANDY JACKSON:
BOY SOLDIER

ANTHONY WAYNE:
DARING BOY

BENJAMIN FRANKLIN:
YOUNG PRINTER

BOOKER T. WASHINGTON:
AMBITIOUS BOY

BUFFALO BILL:
BOY OF THE PLAINS

CLARA BARTON: FOUNDER
OF THE AMERICAN RED CROSS

DANIEL BOONE:
YOUNG HUNTER AND TRACKER

GEORGE CARVER:
BOY SCIENTIST

GEORGE WASHINGTON:
YOUNG LEADER

ISRAEL PUTNAM:
FEARLESS BOY

KIT CARSON: BOY TRAPPER

MOLLY PITCHER:
YOUNG PATRIOT

MYLES STANDISH:
ADVENTUROUS BOY

NANCY HANKS:
KENTUCKY GIRL

PAUL REVERE:
BOSTON PATRIOT

SAM HOUSTON:
BOY CHIEFTAIN

SITTING BULL: DAKOTA BOY

TECUMSEH: SHAWNEE BOY

U. S. GRANT:
YOUNG HORSEMAN

VIRGINIA DARE:
MYSTERY GIRL

*WILBUR and
ORVILLE WRIGHT:*
YOUNG FLIERS

ZEB PIKE: BOY TRAVELER

★ ★ ★ George
Washington

Young Leader

Along the Rappahannock

"Move back! Move back!" shouted the sheriff. "They're about ready to roll!"

The crowd on the shore moved back, but not enough to suit the sheriff. "Do you want to be killed?" he shouted. "Move back!"

The sheriff walked toward the crowd to push some of the people back. He pointed toward the hogsheads, or barrels, of tobacco ready to come rolling down the hill.

"Move back!" the sheriff shouted to the people again. "Move back!"

This time they obeyed. They knew the danger, for they came to Augustine Washington's plantation every year on "Loading Day." Many came from the little town of Fredericksburg, across the Rappahannock River. Others came from plantations round about.

It was a sight to see—those tobacco hogsheads rolling down the steep bank. It was exciting, too. Sometimes a barrel would "go wild." It would get loose from its ropes and go crashing down like a great monster. Faster and faster! Wilder and wilder! And then with a great splash it would plunge into the deep river.

Field hands up on the bank had placed strong ropes around a hogshead. Now they were holding these ropes—ready to roll when their master gave the signal. But Augustine Washington didn't give it.

He wasn't satisfied. He examined the ropes again. Any hogshead that "went wild" was a bad loss for him. The barrels were packed with his tobacco, raised on his Virginia plantations.

They were to be loaded on the vessel waiting at his wharf and taken to England. The tobacco would be sold there, and the Washington family would live this year on whatever money it brought.

No wonder Mr. Washington examined the ropes carefully. No wonder Mrs. Washington watched closely a little distance away.

A little boy watched with her—a slender, handsome boy, tall for his seven years. His hair was a reddish light-brown. His eyes were gray-blue and very keen. He was watching now as closely as his mother.

"Father won't let them roll," he said. "What's the matter, Mother?"

"He's telling the workers something, George. He's very careful. Everything has to be exactly right."

"Oh! I see what it is!" cried George. "He told them to put on their leather gloves."

"He's afraid the ropes will cut their hands," said Mrs. Washington.

"Look!" cried George a moment later. "Father is lifting his hand!"

"Ready!" shouted Mr. Washington. "Roll!"

"Move back!" shouted the sheriff. "Move back! She's coming!"

George almost held his breath until the hogshead was down the bank, across the wharf and aboard the ship. He was as anxious as his parents. And no one was happier than he when the last cask was on the ship.

He hadn't had new boots last winter. Too much tobacco had been lost, both in the field and in the river. But this year everything was just right. There was no bad tobacco, and not a barrel had been lost.

"Now I know I'll get new boots," he told his little sister Betty. "Mother said I could have brass tips, too."

"I'm going to have new shoes," said Betty. "And I'm going to have brass tips if you do."

BOATS PASSING BY

There were boats on the Rappahannock all day long: rowboats, sailboats, sloops, brigs, brigantines, barges. Sometimes there was a sailing vessel from England. There were often trading vessels from Boston and New York.

All these boats passed by Ferry Farm, and the younger Washington children watched them from the bank.

There was George, now seven and one-half years old. There was Betty, one and one-half years younger. And there were the still younger boys, Samuel, John, and Charles.

The older boys, Lawrence and Austin, were away at school in England. They were the sons of Augustine Washington and his first wife.

The younger of these two sons had been named for his father but was called Austin.

George had been born on February 22, 1732. At that time the Washingtons were living on their Wakefield Plantation. This plantation was near the Potomac River.

Later, when George was six years old, they had moved to their farm on the Rappahannock River. This plantation had three names: "Pine Grove Farm," "Cherry Tree Farm," and "Ferry Farm." Most persons called it Ferry Farm, because the ferry to Fredericksburg was under its banks, and also because Mr. Washington owned the ferry.

The passengers were mostly planters from distant plantations. They rode horseback to the river. Some left their horses at Ferry Farm until they returned. Others took their horses with them.

So sometimes the ferryman rowed a skiff and

sometimes a barge. Sometimes he ferried people, sometimes horses, mules, and cattle. But he was always dressed the same—high boots, blue trousers, red flannel shirt, and blue cap.

George said he looked like a king. Betty and the little boys thought he *was* a king, and they were always delighted when he waved at them. Just now he had waved his cap.

"He never did that before," said George.

They were all so excited about this they almost failed to see a pretty sloop that now came sailing by.

"Oh! There's Aunt Mildred's sloop!" cried George. "She's waving at us!"

Then the children waved and waved. Their Aunt Mildred Washington Willis was their father's sister and lived in Fredericksburg.

Soon after came the Travers' brig. And there was Aunt Hannah Ball Travers waving to them. They waved back as long as they could see her.

Presently, the Seldens' sailboat came skimming along. "There's Aunt Mary at the rudder!" said George. "She's waving! Wave—quick!—before she's gone!"

"Where are they all going?" asked Samuel.

"They're out making calls," said George. "It's around ten o'clock, and that's the time they call in the mornings."

"Mother went calling, too," said Betty. "But she went on horseback."

"She'd rather ride a horse if the roads are good," said George.

Then came a beautiful barge rowed by eight strong Negro boatmen. George knew all about that, too. "It belongs to Mr. Fitzhugh," he said. "There's Mrs. Fitzhugh sitting up in front. Her maid is holding a parasol over her head. Can you see her?"

"I can," said Betty. "Is she our aunt?"

"I don't know," said George. "She might be."

"She's waving just like an aunt," said Betty. So they all waved to her till their arms were tired.

It had been a busy morning. But then every day was a busy day with them, for boats were always passing by. And there was always the ferry to watch, and the ferryman who looked like a king.

One day George made up his mind. "Father," he said, "I'm going to be a ferryman when I grow up. And I'm going to wear blue trousers and a red flannel shirt and a blue cap."

"Well, son, we'll see," said Mr. Washington gravely. "We'll see."

At Ferry Farm

GEORGE was a year older now and he was forgetting to watch the river. He had other things to watch—in his own yard, too—a whole street of them.

The cherry trees hid them from the Washington house. A stranger wouldn't guess that little street was there. It was a pretty, shady little street, with little shops and little houses on each side and close together.

There were shops for carpenters, coopers, tanners, shoemakers, blacksmiths, and other workmen.

There were little houses for smoking hams,

salting pork, making candles, spinning, weaving, cooking, washing, sewing, knitting, and a dozen other things.

All the work for the big plantation was done in this street. Besides, shoes and clothing for a big household were made there. It was a big business. Mr. Washington looked after the farm and the shops. Mrs. Washington managed the work in the little houses. George watched it all.

There was so much going on he couldn't make the rounds in one day. There was always something exciting—a young ox that fought his first yoke—a thorn to be taken from a colt's foot—a dog to be shot for killing sheep.

He watched the coopers making barrels and decided he'd be a cooper. Then he watched the carpenters making a dray and decided to be a carpenter. But it would be wonderful to be a blacksmith and hit the anvil with mighty blows!

He couldn't decide.

"You'll have to be all of them if you ever own a plantation," his father said. "You'll have to understand all kinds of farm work."

So George visited some shop every day and watched the work and asked questions. The workmen liked George, and they saw he was really interested. So they explained things and answered his questions.

Before long George was learning the mystery of making a barrel come out round, a horseshoe fit, a boat float, and many other things.

It was more fun than playing, he thought. In fact, the children couldn't get him to play with them now.

He was busy all day long. And he was happy all day long, too.

Then came a change. The workmen stopped talking to him. They showed him plainly that they didn't want him around. And George knew why.

It was the children's fault. Betty and the boys
had begun to follow him about. If they saw him
in a shop, they came in. Then they would race
about, fall down, grab at sharp tools and get in
everyone's way. Of course the workmen didn't
want him, for that meant Betty and the boys.

This morning he was watching the cooper fit
a barrelhead, when in they came. They got
their feet all tangled up in the shavings—on
purpose. They fell down, got up, fell down and

24

threw shavings at one another. They had a grand time, until the cooper put them out—and George with them.

Then they followed him to the blacksmith's. John got too close to a mule. Charles just missed a kick from a horse. Betty threw horseshoes about. Sam tried to touch the red-hot iron. Of course the blacksmith put them out—and George with them.

At the carpenters' they climbed into a boat the men were working on. They wouldn't get out, either. So the men lifted them out, put them out of the shop, and locked the door. And George was put out with them.

At the shoe shop they took the shoemaker's pegs and tangled his thread and chewed his beeswax. He was angry at them. He put them out, and George with them.

Then they ran round and round the smoke-house along with the hounds. And they sniffed the oozing ham fat, for all the world like hound dogs. George was ashamed of them.

After that he saved Betty from falling into a dye vat at the dyers' house.

"You'd have been green all over," he said. And while the children were laughing at that, George slipped away.

He knew a place they couldn't get in, and he was going there just as fast as he could go.

THE KITCHEN HOUSE

The kitchen was a little house all by itself. It was here that George thought he'd be safe from the children.

Mammy Lou was the cook. She wouldn't let George in when he was little like Betty and the boys. But now she didn't seem to mind him.

Of course he was careful not to get in her way when she was cooking at the big fireplace.

26

Everyone was careful not to get in Mammy's way, for she was an extra-good cook.

Mrs. Washington said she was the best in Virginia. Mr. Washington said she was the best anywhere.

Mammy's husband helped her, and so did her six children. And Mammy's word was law with all of them. She was the queen of the kitchen.

She didn't seem to see George when he slipped in. She was too busy scolding Rastus, her eight-year-old.

"Shell those peas in the pan!" she ordered. "The floor isn't the place for them."

"I can't hit the pan, Mammy."

"Do you see that cherry-tree switch in the corner? Its the meanest switch there is."

"I know that," said Rastus.

"Now can you hit the pan?"

"Yes-sum!"

Then the cook turned to George. "I don't

want you messing round," she said sternly. "Get out, Mister George! Get!"

George got. Everyone had to mind Mammy. Just as he went through the door he saw Betty and the boys coming to the kitchen.

Then George Washington made his first retreat. And it was well managed, too. He ran behind the kitchen, behind the salt house, and straight to the cooper's shop.

The coopers were at dinner. So no one saw George as he climbed from a keg to a barrel, from the barrel to a hogshead—and then down into it!

"Betty won't find me this time," he said to himself, "nor the boys either."

DINNER AT THE "BIG HOUSE"

The Negroes called the house where the Washington family lived the "Big House." It wasn't a very big house—neither was it a small house. It had four large rooms and a wide central hall on the first floor. It had a front porch but no great white columns. The front of the house faced the road. The back was to the river.

The dining room was at the back, so its windows looked out over the river. It was a large room with a polished floor. The fine walnut furniture came from England. There were four corner cupboards filled with silver, glassware, and china. It had all come from England, too.

The large table was set now for a family dinner. There was a white linen tablecloth and on it were the blue-and-white everyday dishes. The silver sugar bowl and cream pitcher were on a silver tray at Mrs. Washington's place. The silver carving set was at Mr. Washington's place.

It was a lovely room. And Mary Washington saw to it that her children had lovely manners there. So now they stood behind their chairs, waiting for their parents to sit.

When they were all seated, Mr. Washington looked around. "Where is George?" he asked.

"He ought to be here. He certainly heard the dinner bell," said Mrs. Washington. "I never heard Rastus ring it so loud or so long."

"It could be heard clear across the river," said Mr. Washington.

"I won't have George late to meals," said Mrs. Washington. "It's bad manners."

"Ah, but George is a busy person, Mary. He's always watching the work in the shops. He's beginning to understand it, too."

"I wish he understood what that dinner bell meant," said Mary. "He's old enough."

The door opened then and a procession entered. Pappy came first, in his white uniform. He was followed by all of his six children, each with a dish of food. And each wore a big white

apron that covered shirt or dress, though all were barefoot.

Pappy placed the dishes on the table. Then the children marched out. He stayed to pour the water and pass the food.

Mr. Washington said grace. Just as heads were lifted and eyes opened, in came George.

He had a nice smile for his father and another for his mother as he took his place at the table. "I'm sorry I'm late," he said.

"Didn't you hear the bell?" asked his mother.

"No, I didn't, Mother. I was in a hogshead and I went to sleep. Rastus had to wake me up and tell me it was dinnertime."

"What were you doing in a hogshead?" asked Mr. Washington. "Did you want to see how it was made?"

"No, Father. It wasn't that."

"He was hiding from us," said Betty. "He ran away from us. I saw him."

"George Washington! I'm ashamed of you," said his mother. "Why did you run away from the children?"

Then George told how hard it had been to keep the children from the shavings, the sharp tools, the mule, the horse, and the red-hot iron.

"Oh! That's terrible!" exclaimed Mrs. Washington.

But George wasn't through. There were the boat and the dye vats.

"Ha, ha!" laughed Betty. "I'd be green."

"Ha, ha!" laughed Sam, John, and Charles.

"Stop!" said their father sternly. "Now then, listen to me. Don't you children go near those shops again. It's dangerous. I forbid you to follow George about. Do you understand me?"

"Yes, sir," said Betty meekly.

"Yes, sir," said the others.

"You see, George," said his mother, "they love you. That's why they want to follow you."

"Can't they love me and stay at home?" asked George.

"They can and they will. I'll have a nurse with them after this."

Then Mr. Washington talked about a trip he was going to make to his iron mine up in the hills.

"It's making money now," he said. "We won't have to depend on tobacco after this."

"I'm glad of that," said Mary Washington. "Even after you ship the tobacco it's liable to be lost at sea."

By this time George had finished his meal. So he asked his mother if he could be excused.

"But dinner isn't over," she said. "There's a pie coming."

"The carpenters are ready to test the new boat and I'd like to be there, Mother. If it doesn't float, I'd like to know the reason."

Mrs. Washington was about to say "no." But

when she saw how serious he was, she changed her mind. "Of course you may be excused."

No wonder George Washington loved his mother. And no wonder he loved his father. They understood things.

George skipped happily down the slope toward the river. Suddenly he saw the carpenters working at the edge of the water. They were about to launch the new boat. George broke into a run. He didn't want to miss the launching.

Master Hobby's School

MR. WASHINGTON had just returned from his iron mine, and Mrs. Washington was telling him the news.

"George's vacation is over," she said. "He's been in school three weeks."

"Is he learning anything?"

"He's learning to dance," said Mary Washington with a smile.

"Is that all?"

"Oh, no! He has learned to bow." She smiled again.

"Doesn't Master Hobby teach anything but dancing and manners?"

"Isn't that his hobby?"

Augustine smiled. "I guess it is."

"That's how he got his name," Mary went on. "No one ever calls him William Grove."

"Well, Grove or Hobby, it's his business to teach reading, writing, and arithmetic. That's what he's paid for."

"Oh, George says he hears classes now and then."

"He's no teacher!" exclaimed Augustine.

"He doesn't pretend to be," said Mary. "He only took the school because we couldn't get a teacher. I suppose he's better than no one."

"Very little better. I wish we could send George to a good school."

"There's none near enough. The closest is Mr. Williams' School."

"That's thirty miles from here," said Augustine. "And the road is bad. George couldn't even ride a horse in the winter."

"I wouldn't think of sending him away to board—he's too young. And he's really learning to read, Augustine."

"I suppose he teaches himself."

"He gets it somehow. He's learning some arithmetic, and his writing is very good. His trouble is spelling."

"What grades does he get in spelling?"

"Zero."

"Zero!"

"Every day. Here are two of his papers. I saved them to show you."

Mr. Washington took the papers from his wife. This is what he saw:

Spelling	
George Washington	Corrected by
Oct. 13, 1741	Master Hobby
laff	laugh
hart	heart
mutch	much

blew	*blue*
oyl	*oil*
wunz	*once*

Spelling	◐
George Washington	*Corrected by*
Oct. 14, 1741	*Master Hobby*
meazles	*measles*
mashur	*measure*
blam	*blame*
shour	*sure*
wante	*want*
butt	*but*
soe	*so*
tha	*they*
sutch	*such*

"Well," said Augustine, "I can see by these that George isn't so good in spelling."

"He takes after me," said Mary.

"No indeed! He takes after me."

"I insist. I never could spell."

"None of us can," said Augustine. "Everyone in Virginia spells by sound. I hope someone will write a new kind of book some day—just lists of words with their meanings."

"That would be splendid!" cried Mary. "I'd buy one for George."

"And use it yourself, madam?"

"Yes," said Mary, "you and I both."

Augustine laughed. Then he became serious. "I'm going to teach George the things he has to know," he said. "Where to plant tobacco, and when to plant it; how to cure it, and when to pack it."

"We lost a lot of tobacco last year because it was packed at the wrong time," said Mrs. Washington.

"And we lost a lot of money last year," said Mr. Washington. "George must learn how to run a plantation."

40

"Even if he can't spell," laughed Mary.

"And, I might add, even if he can dance," laughed Augustine.

TOMBSTONES

Master Hobby's school was two miles above Fredericksburg. It was on the same side of the river as Ferry Farm. So George rode horseback unless it was too muddy. Then he had to walk.

The school was in a little house in a churchyard. Master Hobby was allowed to use the house because he took care of the church. He was the sexton, or janitor. In the churchyard there was also a graveyard.

It was so close, the schoolhouse was on the edge of it. So the tombstones were always in sight. But that didn't worry the boys. They forgot these were tombstones. They used them for reading lessons.

They had no readers, so they were glad to have the stones with their names and verses. Some of the boys learned the alphabet by spelling out the names:

W-I-L-L-I-A-M B-R-O-W-N

R-A-C-H-E-L W-I-L-L-I-S

M-I-L-D-R-E-D G-R-E-G-O-R-Y

The older boys liked to read the verse on John Hizer's tombstone:

"John Hizer
The miser
Is wiser—we hope."

They liked the verse on the pirate's tombstone so well they learned it by heart:

"I was a bad pirate.
I'll never deny it.
But it's 'Ho for me!'
Wherever I be."

They learned the "Constable's Verse" by heart, too:

"I'm watching you as you pass by,
I'm watching you with my one eye.
If any wicked come around,
I'll pop right up from out the ground."

Then there were those two verses they said at home just to tease their mothers:

"Here lies William David Kent.
We do not know which way he went."

"Don't cry, don't sigh,
You'll be as I
In the sweet by-and-by."

The boys thought these were very funny. Their mothers didn't know whether they ought to laugh at such things, so they smiled—but only a little, a very little.

43

Master Hobby used the stones for arithmetic problems, too. "They are splendid for subtraction," he said.

1.   Sarah Grimes
        Born 1650   Died 1698
        How old was Sarah in 1657?

2.   John Washington
        Born 1631   Died 1677
          How old was he in 1674?

"Why," said George, "he was my great-grandfather!"

"Never mind that," said the master. "Get the answer at noon from his tombstone!"

Master Hobby's Wig

BUT ONE Friday, the pirate's tombstone was used for something quite different. At noon Lewis Willis saw something hanging on it.

Lewis was George's first cousin because Mildred Washington Willis was Lewis' mother. He was also George's best friend. So, of course, he took George straight to that stone.

"Look at that!" he said. "Isn't that a good joke! It's the master's wig!"

"For goodness' sake!" exclaimed George. "That's a new one! Do you suppose it got wet and he hung it there to dry?"

"It might be. Hope it won't make the pirate

mad," laughed Lewis. "He was a bad one. He said so, himself."

"The constable will take care of him," laughed George. "He's always watching with his one eye."

Just then a sudden breeze blew the wig off the stone. It fell at George's feet. He picked it up and looked at it. He looked at it so long Lewis thought it was time to say something.

"You'd better put it back on the stone. He's likely to come any minute."

"He won't find it there," said George grimly. "I'm going to hide it."

"He'll whip you within an inch of your life."

"If he finds out," said George.

"He'll find out some way. He always does."

"How can he? There isn't a boy in sight. There's no one to tell but you."

"You know I won't."

"I know that, Lewis. I'm going to let old

Hobby worry about his hair for a while. Look how he made fun of mine this morning!"

"I don't blame you for being mad. It made me mad, too, the way he went on."

"What was the matter with my hair? I combed it just before I left home."

"Oh, your hat had mussed it and it stood up a little."

"He had them all laughing at me," grumbled George.

"I know it. Go on and hide his old wig. It will serve him right. Hang it up in a tree."

"The birds would pick it to pieces. He can't afford a new one—he's poor."

"Hang it in the belfry."

"The bats would roost in it."

"Then I don't know where you could hide it."

"I know!" cried George. "I'll put it in the pocket of his black robe—the one he wears to church on Sunday. I know where it is."

"Where?"

"He keeps it in the cloak room."

"Good!" said Lewis. "He'll never think of looking in his own pocket."

The boys crept into the church, down the aisle and back into the cloak room. There hung the deacons' black robes. There was only one short robe, so that, of course, was Master Hobby's. Quickly into the pocket went the wig! Then the boys hurried out and waited for the master with the other pupils.

Presently he came. Straight to the pirate's tombstone he went, and then he faced his pupils. "Well," he said sharply, "where is it?"

No one answered.

Master Hobby spoke again. "Where is my wig? Who took it?"

No one answered.

Then Master Hobby was angry. "Look here," he said, "I'm bound to find out. It was a prank,

of course, but I am willing to overlook it. Once
more—where is my wig?"

No one answered.

Master Hobby was now very angry. "It's the
same as stealing!" he cried. "Is one of you a
thief?"

No one answered.

"Very well then. I shall take you into the schoolroom and examine you one by one. After that you may go home. There will be no school this afternoon."

So one by one the boys went in. And one by one they came out and went home.

George was one of the last boys to go in. Lewis waited for him behind some bushes. "S-sh! George! Over here! Did you tell?"

"Of course not!" said George.

"Ha, ha!" laughed Lewis.

"Ha, ha!" laughed George.

"Do you think Master Hobby suspects us of taking his wig?" asked Lewis.

"No, I'm sure he doesn't," said George. "And I hope he never finds out who did it."

The boys went to their own homes. Neither of them mentioned what had happened in school.

It was Saturday—the day to draw in the large seine. A crowd was watching down on the river shore at "The Fishery." This was Mr. Washington's fishing ground and it was quite a distance from the wharf.

A dozen strong Negro workers were holding the seine ropes. Mr. Washington gave the signal and they began to pull. It was hard work, for the seine was full of herring.

"I'll bet there are at least a thousand," said Lewis. Every Saturday he came to watch the men haul in the seine.

"I'll bet there are at least ten thousand," said George. He, too, was on hand every time the seine was hauled in. Everything about the plantation interested him.

"No, there can't be that many," argued Lewis. "There aren't ten thousand fish in the whole Rappahannock River."

Just then Rastus came up. "Mister George,
the Missus wants you to come home right away.
There's company."

"Who?" asked George.

"I don't know. Joseph told Lucinda, and Lucinda told Melinda, and Melinda told Belinda, and Belinda told me."

"I'll come back, Lewis," said George. Then he started home with Rastus.

"Did the company come in a coach, Rastus?"

"No, sir. There's no coach at the door."

"Did they come in a boat?"

"No, sir. There's no boat at the wharf. And there's no horse at the hitching rack."

"It's none of our kinfolk then," said George.

"No, sir," said Rastus proudly. "Our kin don't walk anywhere ever."

"They live too far away," said George.

They reached the house. George went in, and Rastus waited outside to see what he could see.

George hung up his hat in the hall, smoothed his hair, pulled down his coat, and straightened his stock. Then he went into the parlor.

There sat Master Hobby in a tall, straight-backed chair. He wore his black robe and black skull cap and he looked very solemn. Mrs. Washington looked very solemn, too.

George bowed to the master, then waited.

"George," said Mrs. Washington, "Master Hobby has been telling me about his wig."

George was silent.

His mother continued. "Master Hobby thinks you may have heard something since Friday. He says the boys tell you everything. He says you are their leader."

George was silent.

Then Master Hobby spoke. "I know how it is, George; you don't want to tell on your school-mates. But think of me. I can't appear in church like this. All the other deacons will wear wigs. I can't appear in school like this, either. The boys wouldn't obey me."

Then he turned to Mrs. Washington. "I shall

have to close my school, madam, until my wig is found. I can't afford to, not even for one day. I am a poor man, a very poor man. My school pay is my bread and butter."

George had never seen Master Hobby like this before. There were no angry words now. He was a miserable, unhappy man. And George's heart was touched. He couldn't bear to see the master like this.

"I'll tell you, Master," said George. "I took your wig."

"You!" cried Master Hobby.

"You!" cried Mrs. Washington.

"I hid it. It's in your pocket, sir."

Master Hobby put his hand in his pocket and drew out his wig.

"Well!" he said. "In my own pocket, too!"

"George, why did you take his wig?" asked his mother sternly.

"He made fun of my hair yesterday morning."

"What was wrong with it, Master Hobby?" asked Mrs. Washington.

"Ah, I hardly remember. Oh yes, it comes to me now. His hair hadn't been combed."

"I beg your pardon, sir," said Mrs. Washington. "I saw him comb his hair yesterday morning. But George's hair is like mine. It won't lie flat—it's that kind of hair. Do you wish to make fun of me, sir?"

"Ah, madam, I'm sorry," stammered the master. "I beg your pardon, madam. I beg your pardon, George. I—I can say no more."

Poor Master Hobby had offended one of the great ladies of Virginia. Nor was that great lady through with him. She stood and spoke.

"Master Hobby, while you are teaching the boys good manners, it would be well to mend your own."

"Yes, yes, to be sure, to be sure. Thank you, madam, thank you."

"And, Master Hobby, remember this: my son is not to be made fun of. Punish him if you must, but ridicule him never."

"I shall remember, madam. Good morning, good morning."

Then with bows and more bows, the schoolmaster was gone.

"He'll never make fun of our hair again," said Mary, as she put her arm about her son.

Contests
and Battles

MASTER HOBBY told the truth when he said George was the leader. He was, in school and out.

He was now ten years old but he was as tall as a boy of twelve. And he could do more than two boys of twelve. He was slender but his shoulders were broad. His hands and feet were big and strong—so strong he could throw any of the boys in a wrestling match. He could also swim farther, jump higher, run faster, and lift heavier weights.

Not a boy studied harder. Not one was more truthful. If George said a thing was thus and so, that's the way it was. "He's fair and square," the boys said. "Besides, he's smart; he knows how things should be done."

George planned all their contests. He had everything ready now for the most exciting one of all—the Boys' Raft-Poling Contest. This always drew a large crowd. Merchants closed their stores to go and farmers left their farms.

The rafts were to start from Stingray Island and stop at Fredericksburg, one mile below. They had to stay in shallow water so they could be poled.

The water between the island and the shore was shallow, but there were large boulders in it. These made the current here swift and rough. Only the strong and skillful could pole his raft through.

The boys were ready now and waiting for the signal. They all wore the riverman's dress—high boots, blue trousers, red flannel shirt, and blue cap. There wasn't a weakling among them. They were outdoor boys and they knew how to take care of themselves.

Now the signal was given and the eight rafts pushed off. At once some were caught in the swift current and whirled about.

Their raftsmen went whirling, too, and their long poles with them. The boys were thrown from side to side. They fumbled and stumbled and tumbled. Then one by one they went over-board and swam to the shore.

The crowd roared with laughter. They roared again when other rafts went end-up on rocks. The raftsmen couldn't stand on the slanting floors. They slipped and slid and fell—got up, slipped, slid, and fell again. Finally these boys had to swim to shore.

Only two could pole around the rocks. George was one. And he was the only one who reached Fredericksburg. He was lucky this time.

He wasn't always lucky. Last year his pole had broken and he had been thrown overboard with great force.

Another time his raft had turned over when it hit a rock, and the whirling water had sucked him under the boat. Then a dozen men had pulled off their coats to dive. They had been afraid he wouldn't come up. But his great strength had saved him. He had fought the whirling waters and won.

His strength saved him from many dangers all through his life.

THE SHAM BATTLE

Bad news came from the distant borderland of Virginia. Indians were attacking the settlers and killing them.

The next day all the men in Fredericksburg were drilling. They feared their borderland would be attacked next. George's uncle, Henry Willis, was the captain. He drilled them every day in the late afternoon, and every day George was there watching.

He meant to be ready if trouble came. He learned drills and orders by listening. By asking his uncle questions he learned how to form a company.

So before long George formed a company of boys at school. They chose him for their captain. No one else knew as much about drilling. No one else had bothered to learn it.

They drilled with cornstalks for guns, and their captain kept them at it till they were ready to drop. But they didn't drop. They got better and better, stronger and stronger.

Captain George was strict. Heads had to be held high and eyes kept straight ahead. And he wouldn't permit anyone to talk back to him, not even his cousins.

There were six of them in his company, and they had all obeyed him until one day. Then it was Cousin Johnny Travers who refused.

George had ordered his soldiers to "right face." "Oh! give us a new one!" yelled Johnny.

Captain Washington seized Johnny by his collar and shook him. No one got "funny" with the strong-armed officer after that.

Then came the day of the sham battle. George had brought staves for them to carry instead of cornstalks.

"We'll carry them as we march to the field," he said. "But we'll throw them down as we march on. And remember you are to shove your enemy off the field. Shove with your shoulders, with your arms folded. There is to be no kicking or fighting. No one is to put his hand on anyone."

Then Captain George divided his soldiers into "friend" and "foe" squads, and gave each boy a stave.

When all were ready he gave the order to advance. He thought they looked splendid as they marched forward. They held their heads high and their staves straight. George wished their parents could see them.

In an instant all was changed. George's orders were forgotten. Friend and foe hit with staves and hit to hurt.

"Staves down! Staves down!" yelled the captain, but they didn't even hear him. They were fighting like savages—hitting out right and left.

Then the wounded began to drop out. Faces, arms ,and legs were bloody, bruised and cut. Everyone was mad at someone. In ten minutes every boy had gone home to Mother.

George went home, too, but not to Mother, for he was ashamed. He had failed. His troops had disobeyed him and then they had deserted.

Captain George Washington shed a few tears that night in bed.

Punishment and Reward

THERE was nothing strange about visitors coming to Ferry Farm. Almost every day some lady came to call on Mrs. Washington. But no one ever came before ten o'clock in the morning. That was bad manners.

However, on this Saturday, the day after the sham battle, visitors began coming long before ten, bad manners or not.

Mrs. Fitzhugh came at nine, in her coach-and-six. At fifteen minutes after, a coach-and-four brought Mrs. Hannah Ball Travers. She was Mary Washington's half sister and, of course, George's aunt.

Then came ladies on horseback and ladies in boats. Nearly all of them were George's aunts— the mothers of his cousins. They were also the mothers of the boys hurt in yesterday's battle.

Now George was good in arithmetic, and he could put two and two together as well as any- one. So he decided to hide behind the hedge.

Rastus found him there. "Mister George, they're all in the parlor fussing about you. I heard them plainly under the window."

"What did they say, Rastus?"

"They said you haven't got the sense you were born with. And they asked why you gave the boys staves. Were you fixing to kill them?"

"Is Mother mad, too?"

"Sure is. And she told them she'd take care of you. They needn't worry."

"Is Father there?"

Rastus shook his head. "And you're lucky, Captain. Your ma isn't as strong as your pa."

"She's strong enough."

"Get yourself ready. You sure are bound for the woodshed, Captain."

Then Rastus went to see what he could see and hear what he could hear. And George got himself ready. He knew what was coming, just as sure as two and two make four.

Rastus came back. "Captain, they're all gone. Wouldn't any of them stay to dinner. And the Missus said you were to come to the woodshed. She sent for switches."

George went. His mother was waiting.

"Why did you let the boys use staves?" she asked sharply.

"They looked better than cornstalks."

"It's a wonder someone wasn't killed," said Mrs. Washington. "They're all in bed with cuts and bruises."

"I told them not to use the staves!" cried George. "I told them over and over!"

68

"You might have known they would. You were the leader. It was your business to look ahead and think of everything that might happen. You didn't. So you are to blame."

Mammy Lou came with switches. "Here they are," she said. "I got them from that old cherry tree—the biggest one."

"I wish I'd cut them all down!" cried George.

"I wish to goodness I had! Every last cherry tree on the place!"

"Mammy, go along," said Mrs. Washington. "George, take off your coat."

GEORGE AND THE CHERRY TREE

Mammy Lou came back to the kitchen laughing. She sat down in front of the fire laughing. She kept right on laughing.

"How can you laugh like that when Mister George is getting licked!" exclaimed Rastus.

"I'm laughing at what he said, Rastus."

"What did he say?" asked Belinda.

"He said, 'I wish I'd cut them all down while I was a-cutting! I wish to goodness I had! Every cherry tree on the place!'"

Everyone laughed but Rastus. "Wish he had!" he cried. "Wish he had!"

Again everyone laughed but Rastus. This

70

time they laughed so loud Emmy Jane came in to see what was funny.

Emmy Jane was a new servant and she didn't understand about the cherry tree, so Mammy and Pappy told her.

"I saw the stump of a little tree alongside the big cherry tree," she said. "What did he cut it down for?"

"Just wanted to see if his new hatchet was any good," Pappy said.

"Just wanted to see if it could cut wood," Mammy said.

Emmy Jane was puzzled. "I don't see anything wrong about that. How would he know if he didn't cut something?"

"There was the kindling pile," said Melinda.

"There were the fire logs," said Belinda.

Emmy Jane shook her head. "Kindling pile away back. Fire logs away over. That so?"

"That's so," said the others.

"And right here," said Emmy Jane, "right here at hand is a little cherry tree. Of course he cut it down. Isn't that just natural?"

"It is," said Pappy. "I never blamed him a bit."

"Did he get a licking?" asked Emmy Jane.

"No," said Mammy. "His pa said he was so glad George told the truth he wouldn't lick him."

"Told him!" cried Emmy Jane. "What did he

do that for? Why didn't he just keep his mouth shut? Then his pa might think one of us did it."

" 'Cause George Washington isn't that kind of a low-down, lying person," said Mammy. "He was born honest. And he's going to be honest, as long as he lives."

TWO YOUNG FRIENDS

Rastus slipped out. He loved George dearly and he couldn't bear to have him whipped. He wanted to do something for him, but what could he do? He sat on the woodpile and talked aloud to himself. "He always gives me something when I get a licking. Wish I could give him a calico horse. Pappy says there's nothing in the world that's as pretty."

Rastus sighed. "I've got nothing to give him —nothing. Might tell him about my little fox. Might let him see her. But if I do, I'll lose her."

He was right about that, for pet foxes were not allowed on Virginia plantations. So Rastus sat and sat and thought and thought. At last he said, "Mister George is your best friend. Act like it, Rastus. Act like it."

Then he took his fox from a little pen, put it under his coat and went to the woodshed. He found George there alone—just sitting there looking down at the ground.

"Brought you something to look at, Mister George."

George didn't answer. He didn't even look up.

"Won't let any other folks see it."

Still George didn't answer or look up.

"It's a baby fox, Mister George."

Then George looked at Rastus and jumped up. "A baby fox!" he cried. "Where?"

Rastus opened his coat.

"Oh!" said George. "It's beautiful!"

The little fox was beautiful. Her fur was a

lovely gray, soft as velvet. Her eyes were dark and bright. Her nose was black and her little feet were black, too.

"Where did you get her, Rastus?"

"Heard her crying and went and found the den. There she was all alone and so hungry she was about starved. That's why she let me pick her up. Mostly, they don't; they're wild and scary."

"I suppose its mother was killed in a fox hunt."

"Reckon so. I know this fox wasn't weaned—she won't eat anything. I have to give her milk."

"You'll have to let her go, Rastus. The fox hunters don't like pet foxes about."

"Your pa isn't a fox hunter. We've got no pack of foxhounds."

"No, but he lets his friends hunt here. The scent of a pet fox would throw the dogs off the trail of the wild fox."

"I won't let her out when there's a hunt."
George shook his head. "Father won't let you keep her. He won't even let me have a pet fox."

76

"I know all that. But I just can't give her up."

"Let me hold her."

George tried to take the fox, but it snapped at his hand and clung to Rastus.

"See that!" cried Rastus. "She loves me even though she is wild."

"She doesn't care about that," said George.

"Can't have any pet," continued Rastus, sadly. "They took my dog on account of the sheep."

George felt so sorry for Rastus he didn't know what to do. Then suddenly he knew what he would do. In spite of everything and everybody he would do it!

"Rastus," he said, "you can keep your fox till she can eat meat. I'll see to that. Here's my hand."

The two boys shook hands. And gray-blue eyes smiled into brown eyes.

The whipping was forgotten. Two friends had helped each other.

George's Half Brothers

THERE was great excitement at Ferry Farm one morning. Lawrence and Austin Washington were coming home from England! The ship was sailing up the river now! It would land at the Fredericksburg wharf within an hour.

Some servants were dusting the house again. Others were bringing flowers from the garden.

Mrs. Washington wanted these for the large bedroom on the second floor. In fact it *was* the second floor, and as large as the four rooms and wide hall below. There were three big beds here. George and Sam slept in one. The others were for Lawrence and Austin.

The floor had been polished until it shone, and a fire burned in the fireplace. On the long mantel Mrs. Washington now placed vases of flowers.

Mammy Lou was getting a big dinner. There would be oysters, turkey, chicken, ham, beef, six kinds of vegetables, pickles, jelly, jams, preserves, two kinds of pudding, three kinds of cake, hot biscuits,and hot corn bread.

The table was set with the best china and silver. The tablecloth shone like satin. A great bouquet of yellow roses was in a vase in the center.

Mr. Washington and George were going over to meet the travelers. Boatmen were getting the sailboat ready now. George could hardly wait to get started, he was so anxious to see his older brothers. They had been away since he was six and he couldn't remember them very well.

Both had been in an English college. Lawrence, the older one, had also been an officer in England's war against Spain.

"They are very handsome," Mrs. Washington said that morning. "They look exactly like their father."

"People say I'm handsome, too," said George.

Mary Washington didn't want George to be vain, so she said hastily, "You don't look like your father; you look like me."

"Well," said George, "everyone says you are beautiful."

His mother laughed. "Go along," she said. "Your mouth is full of honey."

George was thinking of this as he waited.

Then Pappy called down from the bank, "Wait! Wait! Don't start her! The Missus says you better take the barge! She says that sailboat won't hold the luggage."

"It will take too long to get the rowers," Mr. Washington called back.

"I got them! They're coming soon as they get into their shirts. Here they are now!"

It didn't take those strong rowers long to get the barge across the river and to the wharf. The minute it landed, two handsome young men jumped into it. Then they were hugging their father and George, and saying how glad they were to get home.

George was surprised. Were those stylish

young men his brothers? Why, they looked exactly like pictures of English dandies.

"It took a lot of tobacco to pay for their clothes," George thought. It did, but it was partly from the plantation that had belonged to their mother, Augustine Washington's first wife.

The rowers carried luggage from the wharf until the barge was almost full. There were trunks, bags, boxes, more trunks, more bags, more boxes. There seemed to be no end to it. But at last it was all on the barge and the Washingtons were on their way to Ferry Farm.

"Did you buy everything in London?" asked Mr. Washington.

The young men laughed and said there were a few things left in the London shops.

They laughed again when they heard about the sailboat. "It wouldn't have held our presents!" said Lawrence.

Then George was as anxious to get home as

he had been to get away. He hoped they would give out the presents as soon as they arrived. Why didn't those rowers hurry? It would be dinnertime when they reached Ferry Farm. Then he would have to wait for his presents.

It was a long journey to George. He was glad when it was over and they were climbing the bank to the lawn above.

Mary Washington was waiting for them with her children. She wore a lovely dress, and the children were dressed in their Sunday best.

Back of them stood Mammy Lou and Pappy with their children. Back of them waited all the Negro servants and field hands.

Lawrence and Austin were delighted to see their stepmother. They said she was prettier than ever and that Betty looked just like her. They said the little boys were handsome.

They hugged Mammy and Pappy. They greeted Belinda, Melinda, Lucinda, Joseph,

Rastus and Ezekiel. They shook hands with the other Negroes and said something to each one.

George thought they would never finish. He wished his father didn't have so many workers. He wished dinner would be late. He wished Mammy Lou would burn something.

But the dinner bell rang exactly on time, two o'clock. There would be no presents now for an hour or two.

George was disappointed, but he soon forgot all about presents. Lawrence and Austin told funny stories and kept everyone laughing.

"They sure are lively," said Mammy Lou, "just like all the Washingtons."

PRESENTS FROM LONDON

Dinner was over. The luggage had been carried up to the big bedroom, and now the whole family was there to see it unpacked.

Lawrence opened a bag and took out a large package. "For you, Mother," he said, "from both of us."

Mary Washington opened the package. "Oh!" she cried. "How beautiful!" It was a red riding habit. It had a long flowing skirt and a tight waist. There was a little black hat to wear with it, a beaver hat with a black plume.

"I'll wear it when I make calls," she said. "And I'll always ride horseback from now on. No more boats and coaches for me."

There was a fine English riding saddle for Mr. Washington. He was very pleased. "I shall go riding with you, my dear; no more boats and coaches for me, either."

There was a red coat and red cap for George to wear fox hunting! There were also shiny leather riding boots. He was so happy he didn't know what to say. But he managed to thank his brothers.

Then Betty was made happy with a little silk parasol. And the little boys were proud of their presents—beaver hats exactly alike.

The presents for Mammy Lou and Pappy and their children would be unpacked later on.

Then the young men unpacked their own clothing. There were blue satin coats lined with red, and red satin lined with blue. And there were lace ruffles, gold buttons, and silver buckles. There were velvet suits, cloth suits, riding clothes, and hunting clothes.

Lawrence had his uniform, too, and everyone begged him to put it on. So to oblige them he took it and left the room.

"S-sh!" whispered Austin. "Lawrence isn't very well. But don't let him know I told you."

"What is the matter?" asked Mr. Washington.

"It's some sickness he got in the war."

"What kind of sickness?" asked Mary. "Don't try to hide it from us, Austin."

"I don't know, Mother. Lawrence doesn't know himself."

"But the war was a year ago!" said Mr. Washington. "Didn't he go to a doctor in London?"

"Oh, yes, indeed! But he didn't get any better."

Then Lawrence came back wearing his fine uniform. He looked so elegant and so grand that everyone was delighted.

George thought he was wonderful. And then and there he knew what he wanted to be.

"I'm going to be a soldier, too," he said.

"Not with my consent," said Mary Washington. "One soldier in the family is enough to worry over."

"Quite enough," said Mr. Washington. "So get that idea out of your head right now, George."

The Fox Hunt

IT SEEMED that everyone in Virginia wanted Lawrence and Austin to visit them, and to come to balls, parties, dinners, and hunts.

But both found time to be with George, even if they had to give up a ball or a fox hunt. They loved him so much they wanted him with them as much as possible.

George's school was out now for the summer, so they took him hunting, fishing, and sailing. They took him to their father's iron mine, and then to his plantations on the Potomac River, Wakefield, and Hunting-Creek Farm.

They always rode horseback, and from the first

the older brothers were astonished at the way George rode. They spoke of it every time.

"Just look at George!" Austin exclaimed again this morning. "He rides as if he had been born on a horse."

"There isn't an English officer who can ride better," Lawrence said.

"I wish our Virginia friends could see him," said Austin. "I've been telling them about him."

"So have I," said Lawrence. "They'll think we're a couple of braggarts."

"Let's show them, Lawrence. Let's take George to the next fox hunt. The hunters won't care."

"I think they'll be pleased. And I know they'll be surprised when they see George riding break-neck after the fox."

"It's a sight to see, Lawrence. I'm proud of the boy."

"So am I, Austin."

Saturday came. George was dressed before daybreak. Of course he wore his shiny leather riding boots, his red coat, and red cap. He was very proud of his hunting clothes from London.

He went first to the kitchen house to see Rastus, but Rastus wasn't there. And Mammy didn't know where he was.

"He ate his corn bread and left," she said.

"I wanted to tell him to keep his fox in your cabin today. We'll be hunting here on Ferry Farm."

"I'll tell him, Mister George."

"The fox is eating meat now, isn't she?"

"Yes, sir. She keeps Rastus busy catching rats and mice."

"She could hunt her own food if she were free, couldn't she?"

"Of course she could. I told him to turn her out. But Rastus can't bear to give her up, seems like."

90

"He'll have to, Mammy. My brothers have bought a pack of foxhounds. They'll be here tomorrow."

"That fox goes tonight, Mister George. Now then, your breakfast is ready. Go and get your brothers."

It was just daylight when breakfast was over. A groom brought up the horses. The red-coated and red-capped Washingtons mounted. Then away they rode to the meeting place, up by Stingray Island.

THE PET FOX MAKES TROUBLE

At the same time a tall, slender Negro boy was walking to this meeting place. It was Rastus. And he seemed to be talking to himself.

"We're both going to see Mister George ride off with them, Beauty. And I'm keeping you under my coat, so the dogs can't smell you."

91

Rastus cut through fields and reached the meeting place first. He hid in brush and waited. Before long the hunters began to come, and they came and came until there were twenty.

"And all after some poor little fox," said Rastus to himself. Just then he saw George. "There he is, Beauty!" he whispered.

The hunters greeted George and said they were glad to have such a fine rider with them. One said he heard that George was "born on a horse." George was pleased, of course.

Then came the Master of the Hounds, and his dogs. The dogs knew what was coming and they were excited and happy. Every one of them loved a race with a fox better than anything in his dog life. At the first sound of the horn they would be running.

Rastus wanted to see the dogs start, so he crept closer and closer. He didn't know a foxhound could scent a fox through his coat.

Suddenly, a dog near the brush sniffed. Then he gave a cry—that long, drawn-out cry foxhounds give when they scent a fox.

Rastus knew what that cry meant. He ran for the nearest tree, the dog at his heels. He could feel the fox tremble under his coat. He was running like a streak of lightning now, and so was the hound. But for once Rastus was lucky. He made the tree, but just by the skin of his teeth.

In another minute the whole pack was under the tree, yipping and yapping.

"They've scented a fox," said Jim, the Master of the Hounds.

"Why it can't be a fox!" said a hunter. "Foxes can't climb trees."

"Gray foxes can and do," said Jim. "I've seen them climb twenty feet or more to get away from the dogs."

"Well, there's something up there," said another hunter. "I can't make out what it is, but I'll take a shot at it."

Then a strange thing happened. A voice was heard up in that tree!

"Don't shoot! Don't shoot!" cried this voice. "I'm up here. I'm a poor boy up a tree!"

George jumped from his horse and ran to the tree. "Is that you, Rastus?" he called.

"Yes, sir, it's me and Beauty."

George turned to the men. "The boy lives at Ferry Farm. He has his pet fox with him."

"What's he doing with a pet fox?" said the Master angrily. "Negroes aren't allowed to have pet foxes. I'll wring his neck for him!"

"Call off the dogs," said George, "and I'll get him down."

When all was safe Rastus came down, scared to death. His knees were shaking. His eyes were full of fear.

"Drop that fox!" said the Master.

"I don't dare," said Rastus. "The hounds will get her."

"No, they won't. I'm going to shoot it. Drop it!"

"Won't!" cried Rastus. "Won't!"

"Why, you impudent rascal!" cried the Master. He raised his whip.

Then George stepped between them. "I told him he could keep the fox till it could eat meat. It was starving when he found it."

Jim lowered his whip but went on talking to Rastus. "You'd better drop that fox, boy. I'm going to shoot it if I have to shoot through your coat."

At that, George took the fox from Rastus and held it. "Don't tell *me* to drop this fox!" he said angrily.

Lawrence and Austin jumped from their horses and went quickly to their brother's side.

"No one's going to touch this fox or this boy

either," said George. "I will take it to the woods tonight and free it. I give you my word."

Then the courtly Lawrence spoke. "I am sorry, gentlemen, that my family has caused so much trouble. And now, if you will excuse us, we will not hunt today. We must get our boys and their fox out of your way."

Lawrence mounted and helped Rastus up behind him. Austin and George mounted. All touched their caps politely to the hunters and were on their way back to Ferry Farm.

George's Studies

GREAT changes had come to the Washington family. A year ago, when George was eleven, his father died.

After that Lawrence married and went to his plantation on the Potomac River. Then Austin married and went to his plantation, also on the Potomac.

George himself had made a great change. He was now in Mr. Williams' school thirty miles away. Austin's farm was near the school, so George lived with him.

Master Williams was a very fine arithmetic teacher, and George learned rapidly. He loved it and he loved to keep accounts. The master praised George's work to Austin.

"There isn't a better student in my school," he said. "And there isn't one who can show such a neat account book."

A year or so later a new school was opened in Fredericksburg. The master, James Marye, was an educated gentleman from France. He could even give his pupils college studies.

Mary Washington wanted George at home, so she was glad to send him to the Marye school. It was expensive, but crops had been good and she could afford it.

Lewis Willis went to Mr. Marye, along with several of George's other cousins.

George studied Latin, English grammar, spelling, writing, bookkeeping ,and arithmetic. He did as well as the others in everything. In arithmetic he was far ahead of them, thanks to Master Williams.

Since February, when he was thirteen, he had been taking college work in mathematics. He was now studying algebra and surveying.

He loved surveying. No other study was half so interesting to him. He couldn't get enough of it.

"You couldn't study anything more important," said Master Marye. "There are millions of acres of land in Virginia that have never been surveyed. The owners don't know where their land begins or ends. You should have all the work you can do as soon as you are ready to do it."

The boys had to play their games without George after that. He studied before school, after school, and even at noon.

"You aren't a bit of fun any more," Lewis Willis grumbled. "You've always got a book under your nose."

Samuel Washington grumbled, too. "He's like

that at home. I can't get him to play. He studies all evening and after we've gone to bed. You can't get a word out of him."

Samuel was now in the Marye school also, but he studied only when he couldn't get out of it. Mary Washington was wasting her money sending him.

George paid no attention to the boys' grumbling. "I don't have to be any fun," he said. "There's Betty."

George's sister's name was really Elizabeth, but everyone called her Betty. She was now twelve years old and she was very lively. Her cousins all said she was "lots of fun." She was a handsome girl and looked like George. "She's the living image of George," people said.

Sometimes Betty would put on George's hat and coat. Then she would pretend that she was George, doing this and that. She would act it out and make it very funny.

101

She might show George mounting a horse or riding after a fox or studying.

Or she might show him poling a raft that had gone end-up on a rock. Then her slippings and slidings made everyone roar with laughter.

They roared again when she showed George whirling about on a raft caught in the current. George himself had to laugh. And so did Mary Ball Washington.

"It's as good as the theater," said Aunt Mildred.

"It's even better," said Aunt Hannah.

Betty was now in a Dame's school in Fredericksburg. Her two brothers rowed her over and back every day. She always held a little parasol over her handsome head. And she was most careful that no water splashed on her pretty school dress and that no mud was on her neat calfskin shoes.

This morning she was telling her brothers

about her studies. "I have reading, spelling, writing, English, French, and embroidery," she bragged.

"What! No arithmetic?" exclaimed George.

"Of course not," said Betty. "A girl doesn't need arithmetic."

"What about surveying?" teased George. "Why don't you take that?"

"Why don't you take embroidery?" teased Betty.

"I might," George answered. "I'm going to take music lessons."

"You are!" exclaimed Betty. "Did Mother make you?"

"No, I asked her if I could. I like music and I want to play the harpsichord."

"Then I'm going to take music lessons, too," said Betty.

"You don't have to do everything I do, Betty, even if you do look like me."

"Ha, ha!" laughed Samuel.

"I don't think that's funny," said Betty.

"But, Betty, you can pretend you're George playing the harpsichord."

"Oh!" cried Betty. "That will be a good one! I'll show George taking music lessons—that will make everyone laugh."

GEORGE'S COPYBOOK

George was very careful with his copybook work. He copied the sentences the master gave exactly. Not one word was carelessly written. Not one letter was carelessly made.

Master Marye was so pleased he took George's book home with him to show his wife.

"I've never seen such careful work," he said. "Not even in France."

"It is beautiful!" said Mrs. Marye. "His handwriting is clear and exact. He must have a clear and exact mind."

"He has," said Mr. Marye. "I believe George Washington will make a great man—a leader of other men. He has the kind of mind a leader should have."

"That may be true, James, but he'll spend his life going to fox hunts and parties, just like all the rich young men of Virginia."

"George isn't rich."

"His brothers are, and they both married very rich girls. Besides, he has many wealthy relatives."

"That is true, but George never gives it a thought."

"He will when he's older. He'll be invited everywhere—to dinners, balls, and hunts. He can't get away from that kind of a life. He was born into it."

"I'm afraid you're right, but I hate to think it. He's one boy who could do things if he had a chance. He could make a splendid surveyor. He takes to that like a duck to water."

"Swimmingly?" smiled Mrs. Marye.

Mr. Marye smiled. Then he became serious. "Well," he said, "they can kill George's chance to be useful. But there's one thing they can never take away from him—these Rules of Conduct in his copybook."

"Let me look at it again, please. I noticed only his writing before."

Mr. Marye gave her the book. She read it for a moment. "James!" she exclaimed. "These are the very Rules I wrote in my copybook when I was a schoolgirl in France!"

"Of course," her husband replied. "They are the French Rules of Conduct. I put them into English for the boys."

"I want to read every one of them. I loved them."

"Please read them aloud," said Mr. Marye.

Mrs. Marye began to read:

"In the presence of others, do not sing to yourself with a humming voice; nor drum with your fingers or feet.

"Sleep not when others speak.

"Sit not when others stand.

"Speak not when you should be silent.

"Walk not when others stop.

"Turn not your back when speaking to others.

"Let your voice be pleasant at all times.

"Show not yourself glad at the misfortunes of another.

"The best seat by the fire is always for the newcomer.

"Read no letters, book ,or papers in company. But should that be necessary, you must ask leave.

"Come not near the books or writings of anyone so as to read them.

"Take nothing up from another's desk.

"Look not when another is writing a letter.

"The young must stand until older ones are seated.

"They must stop at a door to give way for older folk to pass.

"Speak no ill of anyone.

"Treat all as you would yourself be treated."

Mrs. Marye closed the copybook. "You are right, James. No one can ever take good manners away from George, if he lives by these Rules. But there were more, as I remember them."

"Oh, there are a hundred more! The boys have each taken one copybook home."

"I hope it won't make their parents angry," said Mrs. Marye.

"Angry? Why?"

"Because you, from France, are teaching their children manners. These Virginians have beautiful manners themselves, as beautiful as any of the French."

"Ah yes, but their children haven't. They have not taught their children good manners."

That very night Mary Washington called John to her bedroom.

"John," she said gravely, "I want to read something to you from George's copybook. 'When at table neither spit, cough, nor blow your nose, unless it is necessary. ''

"But it was necessary," said John. "I had to blow it."

"Then you should have left the room. See that you do the next time."

That very night, over in Fredericksburg, Mrs. Mildred Washington Willis called her son to her bedroom.

"Lewis," she said, "I want to read you something from your copybook. 'Do not spit forth

seeds or fruit stones or anything, upon a dish; neither spit them upon the floor.' "

Lewis was ashamed. He looked down at the floor. "I forgot," he said.

"I've told you to lift your spoon to your mouth, then put the seeds on your plate, *from the spoon.* Understand?"

"Yes, of course, but I see other boys spit things out all the time."

"I wish you didn't know any other boys!" said Mrs. Willis.

That night, also, Mrs. Hannah Ball Travers called Johnny to her bedroom. She then read this aloud from his copybook: " 'Scratch not at table. Neither kill, in the sight of others, any kind of vermine, such as fleas, lice, or ticks.' "

"I couldn't help it, Mother," said Johnny. "I had to scratch. I found the tick, too."

"You didn't have to mash it at the table," said Mrs. Travers. "You spoiled your father's supper and mine, too. After this, take your tick and leave the room."

"I'll try to remember," said Johnny.

"You'd better remember," said his father sternly. "And everything else in that copybook, too."

"Yes, sir," said Johnny meekly.

Mrs. Marye had no cause to worry about the Virginians being angry at Mr. Marye.

Lawrence Plans
for George

ONE AFTERNOON George was astonished to see Pappy talking to Master Marye. He was still more astonished when the master told him he was to go home with Pappy at once.

"Mister Lawrence has come," Pappy explained, as they went down the bank. "He asked the Missus to send for you."

"Has anything happened?"

"Not so far as I can see."

"Is Lawrence all right?"

"As far as I can see, he is."

"Then why did they send for me? It's never happened before. Didn't you hear anything?"

"Your brother said he'd just come from the Governor's Palace at Williamsburg. What was he doing there, Mister George?"

"He's one of the lawmakers of Virginia now. He had to go there to talk to the Governor."

"About the laws for horse thieving, and not going to church Sundays?"

"Yes, that's part of it. There're a lot of other laws, too."

"Then why is the Governor talking about you?"

"About me!" exclaimed George. "Why, the Governor doesn't know I'm on earth!"

"He does now," Pappy said. "Your brother told him."

"You didn't understand, Pappy."

"Maybe I didn't. But my ears are pretty good."

By this time they had reached the river and Pappy had untied the skiff.

114

"I'm going to row," said George.

At the same time Lawrence Washington was telling his stepmother about the new house. "I'm building it on the highest part of the bank," he said. "We can see the Potomac River for miles."

"I know the place," said Mrs. Washington. "The view from there is lovely, the best on Hunting-Creek Farm."

"Not Hunting-Creek any more, Mother. I've given it a new name—Mount Vernon."

"I can understand the Mount, for the bank there is a mount. But why Vernon?"

"In honor of Admiral Vernon."

"Why, of course! You were on his ships when you went to the war with Spain. I remember now. Well, it's a beautiful name, Lawrence. I hope no one will ever change it."

"I hope it will last as long as the house," said Lawrence, "and I'm building a good one."

"Is it larger than the old house?"

"Much larger. We have so much company, I had to build extra rooms."

"I hope you won't have the bad luck Cousin Emma had. She invited a friend for three weeks. The lady stayed three years."

Lawrence laughed. "I know a better story than that," he said. "Mr. Van Horn invited his uncle for one day. He stayed thirteen years."

They were laughing at this when George came in. He was now a big boy of fourteen, all hands and feet. But he knew what to do with them. Mr. Hobby had taught him that. He knew how to greet his brother, too, and ask after his health.

"Oh, I'm pretty well these days," said Lawrence, "pretty well, thank you."

"I was afraid something had happened when Pappy came for me," said George.

"Something has happened," said Lawrence. "I heard some news at the Palace yesterday, and I came straight to tell you."

George was astonished again. "You came to tell me!" he exclaimed.

Lawrence continued: "The Governor has decided to buy a large tract of land from the Indians—a million acres or more. It's on the other side of the Blue Ridge Mountains. It will be divided into small tracts and sold to new settlers. Now do you see where you come in?"

"It will have to be surveyed!" said George.

"Of course. I've already spoken to the Governor about you, and I believe he will appoint you. He wants strong surveyors. A weakling wouldn't last long in the wilderness."

"Oh, but I couldn't, Lawrence! I don't know enough. I'm not through the course."

"You will be by the time the land is bought. It will take a year at least. Indians never sell their land in a hurry. And you won't be the only surveyor. There will be older men with you. You'll be well paid, too."

117

"There's nothing I'd like better," said George. "You don't object, do you, Mother?"

"I'd be very glad for you to get it," said Mrs. Washington. "Lawrence had my consent before I sent for you."

"I'll study harder than ever," said George.

"I think practice will do you more good," said his brother. "Talk with Mr. Marye and arrange it. Begin tomorrow here at home."

"I couldn't measure this big farm, Lawrence."

"I don't mean the whole plantation. Begin with the vegetable garden, the potato field, and the turnip patch. Then work out the boundary lines of the cornfield, the wheat field, tobacco fields, and pasture."

"I'll do it!" cried George. "I'll get Rastus to carry my chain and stakes."

A head suddenly appeared at the parlor window. "I'll carry them, Mister George!" cried Rastus. "I'll carry them till kingdom come!"

118

George didn't waste any time. He measured everything. He worked slowly, for he wanted his measurements right. He then made maps of every garden, field, and pasture. And he set down the figures to show the size of each piece of land.

Mr. Marye examined his work and said it was correct and very well done.

Rastus was in heaven. "Mammy," he said, "I'd much rather carry those chains than eat."

Elizabeth Washington was in heaven, too. It gave her a fine chance to act like Surveyor George.

One day she put on George's hat and coat and went to the tobacco fields. Little Ezekiel, Mammy's seven-year-old, whom everybody called Zeke, carried the chain and stakes.

Betty had told him just what to do and say. He was proud enough to burst.

Surveyor Elizabeth pretended to measure the

field. She ran about acting important. She motioned Zeke to the left. He went, dragging his chain. Then she motioned rapidly right, left, back, forward, right, left, back. Poor Zeke was dizzy from running back and forth, but it made everyone laugh.

Of course there was a crowd there. There always was when "Miss Betty acted." Mrs. Washington let everyone stop work for a little while.

At last Betty ordered Zeke to drive the stake there where he stood.

"Can't!" he said. "Can't!"

"Why can't you?" asked Betty.

"There's a big tobacco worm right here." Then Ezekiel rolled his eyes and pretended to be scared.

Everyone laughed at that. They knew that Zeke had been killing tobacco worms right along, hundreds of them. That was his work.

"Kill it, Zeke! Kill it!" Betty ordered.

120

"I'm scared!" yelled Zeke. "It's looking at me!"

"Bring it to me," ordered Betty. "I dare it to look at me."

Zeke carried the worm to Betty. She looked at it, screamed,and ran from the field.

That made everyone laugh, because tobacco worms were as common there as flies.

George had slipped up to watch. And when Betty showed him running away from a worm, he laughed harder than anyone. The Washingtons loved a good joke even if it was on them.

A CHIEF PLANS FOR HIS TRIBE

Over the Blue Ridge Mountains, an Indian chief was talking to his people. At times he showed anger. At other times, sorrow. But whether angry or sorrowful, his words were to change the plans of a boy surveyor.

121

The boy didn't know this. He was fifteen now, and he had finished his course in surveying. He had finished school, too. He was now *George Washington, Surveyor*.

He surveyed his uncle's land in Fredericksburg. He surveyed land for his neighbors. So he made a little money, now and then. But it wasn't enough to keep him going. He longed for that big job he was to get from the Governor. He'd have plenty of money then.

He planned what he would buy with it. He'd get presents for everyone in the family—and for Mammy's family, too. Rastus should have a new suit. Then he would get a suit for himself—one good enough to wear at Mount Vernon.

And so this boy planned and planned. But the Indian chief was planning, too.

"We must not sell our land to white men," he told his people. "We have given them too much now. They have come to the foot of these moun-

tains. They have cut down our forests for their cabins and fields. There is almost no game for our hunters. We have trouble now to feed our tribe. What will it be when more white men come?

"If we let them cross these mountains, where then shall we go?

"They say we can go west. But many tribes own the land to the west. North and south, friendly tribes own the land. I ask you again, where then shall we go? Where shall we place our wigwams?"

He paused a moment. Then he went on: "Harken to me, my people—I will tell you. There is no place for us to go—no place on this earth. Braves, warriors, the white man waits for our answer. Shall we sell him our land?"

The braves and warriors jumped to their feet. "No!" they shouted. "No! No!"

Lawrence brought the news to Ferry Farm.

124

"The Indians have refused to sell," he said. "So that land won't be opened up to settlers."

It was a blow to George. "I had counted on it," he said. "There were things I wanted to buy."

"George," said Lawrence, "I'd like you to survey my land at Mount Vernon. There're over two thousand acres and I don't know where they begin and where they end."

"I'll be glad to survey your land, Lawrence. I'll try to find out how far your land extends. I've worked hard at surveying, and should know what to do. You may count on me to help."

"Then come home with me today."

"Oh, I couldn't—not just now, anyway."

"Why not? Do you need him, Mother?"

"No. I'd like him to go with you."

"There you are, George. Get your things."

"But you don't understand, Lawrence. I haven't any good clothes. I haven't a single suit I could wear among your friends."

"I'll see to that," said Lawrence. "Go to the tailor in Fredericksburg and get what you need. Charge the bill to me."

"No, no, Lawrence!" said Mary Washington quickly. "I can't let you do that. I intend to get some clothes for George as soon as the money comes in from the tobacco."

"That will be four months, at least," said Lawrence. "I don't want to wait that long."

"If George didn't grow so fast, he'd have clothes," said Mrs. Washington. "I bought two good suits for him less than a year ago."

"Sam can wear them," said George.

Lawrence smiled. "I want George well dressed when he comes to Mount Vernon. He'll meet people there who are large land owners. They may want surveying done, too."

"There is that side of it," said Mrs. Washington. "Everyone in Virginia judges a man by the way he dresses."

126

"That's just it," said George. "They wouldn't think I knew a thing about surveying, if I went in this suit."

"I'm sure they wouldn't," said Lawrence, "not if that suit is your best."

"It is," said George. "You can see for yourself, Lawrence. The breeches are too short and too tight; my coat is too small all over."

"You will need four suits," said Lawrence. "One for big dinners and parties. That should be satin and of a light color. Get a darker one of velvet for Sundays, and a dark cloth for every day. Then you will need a surveying or work suit of some kind. Ask the tailor about that."

"You'll make a young fop out of him," said Mary Washington. But she was pleased just the same.

"Don't worry about that," said Lawrence. "George is too level-headed to become a fop."

"You are very good to me, Lawrence," said

George. "I'm very grateful to you. But I'll pay for the suits, myself, with the money I earn surveying."

"Not this time, George," said his brother. "I want to do this. I don't do enough for you. But I'm having to watch my money now."

"Too much company?" asked smart Mary Washington.

"That's it, Mother. They're eating me out of house and home."

"It's been done before," said Mrs. Washington. "Half the planters in Virginia are in debt because of it. But it won't happen here."

Lawrence smiled. "Oh, but you don't give hunting parties, Madam Washington."

"No," said madam. "I want something for George and the children."

Lawrence left soon after that, and George started for the tailor's.

George Orders New Suits

"No, NO!" cried Dobbs, the tailor. "I cannot do it! I cannot touch your suits this month or next. I have too much work ahead."

"But I need them!" George Washington exclaimed.

"That's what they all say. You'd think no one had anything to wear from the way they talk."

"It's true, Mr. Dobbs. I have to go to Mount Vernon."

"Everyone always has to go some place. Just now, it's the Governor's ball at the Palace in Williamsburg, next month. I've a dozen suits to finish for that."

"Every one of those men has a dozen fine suits at home," said George bitterly.

"No doubt of that," said Mr. Dobbs. "But they must have the latest fashion for the Governor's ball. Vests are a little longer this year, and breeches are a little fuller."

"Mr. Dobbs, look at the suit I'm wearing."

Mr. Dobbs looked. "It's two sizes small," he said. "A good-looking boy like you shouldn't go about in such things."

"I won't get any work if I do."

"What kind of work?"

"I'm going to survey the Mount Vernon plantation for my brother. Then I'm hoping to get other surveys from his friends."

"I've seen you about with your instruments. Do you like that work?"

"I love it. I could measure lots all day long. I never get tired of it."

"That's the way I like to hear a boy talk."

"If you could make only one suit now—say the work suit——"

"I'll do it, my boy! If you tell me you want it for a ball, no, I cannot. But for work, that is different. I like boys who try to get ahead. That's the way I was when I was a young man. I wanted to get to the top of my trade. And I did. I had one of the best shops in London."

"And you left all that! You came over here to this little town!"

"Yes," said William Dobbs, shortly. "Yes, I did."

George felt Mr. Dobbs didn't want to talk about that. He was right. At once the tailor was saying, "Well, my boy, I might see my way to begin your suits in a month's time."

"That's much better than two months," said George with a smile.

"Let's begin with your everyday suit. What kind of cloth do you want and what color, please?"

"I should like wool cloth of a dark plum color, I think."

"Yes, that is good taste. Now what for your best suit, please?"

"Blue satin, sir, light blue. And I'd like the coat lined with white satin."

"The blue will become you. It will make a handsome suit. Have you thought what you would like for your second-best suit?"

132

"I had thought of green velvet, light green."

"No, no, never! Not with your sandy hair and complexion!"

"What color would you suggest?"

"Dark blue velvet would be good for you."

"That is all right," said George. "Now, I don't know what to have for surveying."

"I know the very thing for that. I will make you an Indian work suit out of buckskin. The trousers will be fringed on the outside seams. The coat, or hunting shirt, will come down over them. It will be fringed, also, and have a belt. How would you like that?"

"Are you sure it will be good style?"

"I have just made one for the cousin of Lord Fairfax."

"Oh!" exclaimed George. "Mr. William Fairfax!"

"Yes. He wanted it for some kind of work he's doing on his cousin's plantation."

"I know what it is—my brother told me. Mr. Fairfax is surveying his cousin's land. He's a good surveyor. He studied in England."

"I'm glad to hear of a rich man who isn't above work," said William Dobbs.

"I'd like the Indian work suit, sir."

"Very good. I will measure you in just one month from today. Come early in the morning."

"You are very kind, sir."

"I like to see a boy get ahead," said the tailor.

WILL THE TAILOR TELL?

The day before the month was up, one of the Washingtons came to the tailor shop. But it wasn't George—it was his younger brother, Samuel.

"Mr. Dobbs," he said, "George sent me over to tell you that he doesn't want his suits made."

"What's that?" cried the tailor.

134

"He said to tell you he's sorry, and he hopes you haven't cut into your cloth."

"A nice time to be changing his mind," grumbled the tailor. "Suppose I had cut my cloth? What then?"

"George said he'd pay you."

"Well, I haven't, and that's good luck for him. What made him change his mind?"

"He's not going to Mount Vernon to survey. He's going to sea."

"To sea!"

"His ship will land here today, sir. George has to go aboard at once. He's packing his trunk now."

"Why didn't he let me know sooner?"

"He wasn't sure of going till this morning. Lawrence just brought the letter from the captain of the ship."

"Who managed that plan—your brother Lawrence?"

"Yes, sir. He thought the sea would be better for George than surveying."

"But why? Why?" cried Mr. Dobbs. "Did he think it would give George a chance to become a Naval officer?"

"Yes, sir."

"It won't!" cried the tailor. "There's been many a young man who thought that. But the most of them were disappointed. Tell George he'll be sorry to the end of his life!"

"Yes, sir. Good day, sir." And young Sam left the shop. "I'll not tell George a word of it," he said to himself, "not one word. What does Dobbs know about the sea? He's nothing but a tailor. He's never been an officer like Lawrence."

At this very moment the tailor was talking to his wife. "Jenny, I ought to stop it."

"They won't listen to you, William. Mrs. Washington thinks Lawrence knows best."

"Pooh! Lawrence was on a ship once for a

136

month or so. And then he was an officer with the Virginia troops going to that war with Spain. That's quite a different thing from going to sea as a sailor."

"Very different," said Mrs. Dobbs.

"Lawrence knows nothing about the cruelty of ship captains. No one here knows. Virginia men don't go to sea. They are river folk and farmers. They don't talk about sailors and ships. They talk about tobacco and land."

His wife nodded. "They ought to know that many of these captains treat their crews badly."

"They do," said the tailor. "George will be beaten and starved just as my brother was."

"Jim was a skeleton when he ran away and came to us," said Mrs. Dobbs.

"I don't want any boy to suffer so. I've taken a liking to George. He's an honest upstanding boy. I hate to see his life ruined. It's my duty to warn Mrs. Washington."

"No! No, William! You don't dare. She'll be sure to ask you for proof."

"I don't have to tell her about Jim."

"She'll get it out of you. They say she's very smart."

"No one could make me tell that Jim Boyd is my brother—and a deserter."

"They'd take the ferry away from him if they knew!"

"They'd do worse than that. They put deserters in jail."

"Then you'd go, too! You hid him in London! You brought him with us to America!"

"Yes, the constable would jail us both, if he knew. But how's he going to know?"

"Mrs. Washington——"

"I am sure I can trust her. She'd be grateful to me for telling her the truth."

"But she might think it her duty to have a deserter punished."

138

"Yes," said the tailor thoughtfully, "she might. But someone ought to save that boy."

"S-sh," whispered Jenny. "There's a customer coming now. Don't let him hear us. We'll talk about this after he leaves."

FAREWELL TO GEORGE THE SAILOR

It was afternoon of the same day. Again company was coming to Ferry Farm. Uncles and

aunts came by coach and boat; cousins came on horseback and neighbors came on foot.

This time it wasn't to get George off to the woodshed. No indeed! This time it was to get him off to sea. It was a farewell to George the Sailor. His trunk had already gone. It was now on the wharf in Fredericksburg.

Mammy Lou had baked eight big cakes. Each one was George's favorite. They were being served now by Pappy in his white uniform.

Mrs. Mary Washington was pouring tea. Betty was passing the cups. And everyone was saying what a great chance it was for George.

"Just think, George," said Lewis Willis. "It won't be any time till you're an officer in the Royal Navy. I wish I had your luck!"

"He'll get to see the King and Queen!" said Betty. "I wish I were George."

"He'll get to see London and Paris," said Johnny Travers. "I wish I were George."

George was as proud as a peacock. He could see himself in his officer's uniform, pacing the deck, and giving orders.

Just then Rastus came to the hall door. "The ship is in!" he shouted. "And some sailors are rowing over here in a boat! They're almost to the landing now!"

"They're coming for you, George," said Lawrence.

"Can I help with your bag?" asked Austin.

"No, thank you," said George. "I have a few more things to pack."

He left the room quickly and the others went out to the bank, all but Mrs. Washington. She waited to tell George a last good-by.

Presently Mammy Lou came in. "Missus," she said, "the tailor from over the river has come to see you. He's waiting on the porch."

"Tell him to come some other time. I can't see anyone now."

"He says it's mighty important."

"I suppose he wants to talk about the suits George ordered. Tell him to wait till the ship has sailed."

"Yessum." Mammy Lou went out. But it wasn't a minute till she was back. And the tailor followed her.

"Madam Washington!" he cried. "I have to see you *before* that ship sails! Your son must not go to sea! I have certain things to tell you! I beg you to listen now!"

"Be seated, Mr. Dobbs," said Mrs. Washington. "Mammy, close the door as you go out."

Ten minutes later George came in. He wore his cloak and carried his hat and traveling bag.

His mother was alone, but she was reading a letter that a messenger had brought.

"I'll have to go now, Mother."

"George—I've changed my mind. I don't want you to go to sea."

"Mother! You can't change now! Why, my trunk's on the ship by this time."

"I'll send for it, George. I have just heard certain things about a sailor's life at sea. Mr. Dobbs came just now to tell me. He said the captains are usually very cruel."

"Oh, that's just gossip," said George. "It isn't going to keep me at home. What does a tailor know about the sea?"

"More than you would think. He has known boys who went to sea—one was a relative."

"Well, that's different, but that doesn't prove my captain would be cruel to me."

"That isn't all, George. I have just received a letter from my brother in England."

"Oh! From Uncle Joseph!"

Mrs. Washington nodded. "It came on the ship. You know I wrote Joseph about your going to sea. I asked his advice because he lives close to sailors and ships."

"Yes, I know——"

"Well, his words prove that the tailor told me the truth. He says you will be beaten and starved and treated worse than a dog."

"I won't be a sailor long. I'll be an officer."

"He says that is impossible. He says there are many young men in England who are willing to pay a large sum to be made officers in the King's Navy."

144

"We couldn't do that," said George.

"No, and even if we could, we are too far away to manage it, Joseph says. He says you'll be better off to learn a trade."

"I already know a trade. I'm a pretty fair blacksmith right now."

"There's another reason I don't want you to go, George—and that's Lawrence. He's likely to need you before long, if he doesn't get better."

"Why, is he worse?"

"Yes, he's coughing more. He may have to go to a warmer climate. If he does, I'd like you to go with him."

"I'd want to go! Look what he's done for me!"

"He's been like a father to you, George."

Mrs. Washington stood. "Please read the letter, George. I must write a note to the master of the ship and tell him you're not sailing with him."

Dangerous Work

ANOTHER month had passed and George's four new suits were ready. But Mr. Lawrence Washington wasn't ready. The Governor would want him in Williamsburg for some time, maybe two months longer.

The day that news came, George heard more news. Jim Boyd, the ferryman, told him he was leaving. Mr. Dobbs had bought a farm back in the borderland, and Jim was going to run it.

"I'm tired of the ferry, anyway," he said. He didn't say he was tired of being scared all the time for fear some sailor would know him.

So now there was a new ferryman: a tall,

strong, sandy-haired young giant of fifteen years —George Washington, by name.

He knew that many people in Virginia thought gentlemen should not do hard work. But George liked to work with his hands. He was a pretty good blacksmith now. He was a fair carpenter, too, and he could make a barrel as well as the cooper.

So why shouldn't he ferry the boat? He wanted to make some money—in fact, he needed to make it. Crops had been bad for two years. There was very little money now at Ferry Farm. Mary Washington was having a hard time to feed her big household.

All the relatives knew that, but still they didn't like the idea of George working. His Aunt Mildred said she wouldn't allow Lewis to be a ferryman. Lawrence said it just wouldn't do. Austin said the same thing. But that didn't change George's mind, or his mother's either.

147

"I told you you could run the ferry," she said. "Let them talk."

George looked handsome in his ferryman's outfit: high boots, blue trousers, red flannel shirt and blue cap. And there was a pistol in his belt!

"You'd better carry a pistol," Jim Boyd had said. "I always went armed."

George had been surprised. "I can't understand that," he said. "Your passengers were only planters."

"Not always," Jim had answered. "Sometimes they were horse thieves and gamblers and runaway servants. If they thought I knew them or suspected them, they'd have shot me."

"I'd be afraid of a runaway servant," George had said. "I've heard they were dangerous."

There had been no trouble as yet, but George was always on the lookout. "No one is going to take me by surprise," he told his mother.

Late one afternoon some riders wanted to be

148

ferried across the river. They had to take their horses, for they were riding out to the border-land.

Rastus wanted to help with the barge, but George sent him back. "Tell Mother I'll not be home for supper. It's late now, so I'll eat at Aunt Mildred's."

The members of the Willis family were always glad to see George. Every one of them loved him—even Henry, the big white indentured servant, who waited on the table.

There was a good supper—there always was at Aunt Mildred's. The silver tea set, the white linen cloth, the china,and the flowers made the table lovely, as usual. Henry wore his white uniform, as usual.

The family was as lively as usual. But something was wrong. George noticed that right away. For a moment he couldn't tell what it was. Then suddenly, he knew. It was Henry!

149

The big servant didn't act like himself—he was nervous. He spilled water when he poured it. He could hardly pass the plates, his hands trembled so badly.

"What's the matter with Henry?" George asked Lewis when they were alone.

"I can't make him out," Lewis answered. "He's been acting queerly for a couple of weeks. Everyone has noticed it."

"Do you suppose he's getting ready to run away? They say servants always act queerly just before."

"Henry wouldn't run away," said Lewis. "Just so he gets enough to eat he's satisfied."

THE RUNAWAY

It was dark when George reached the river shore. He was untying his barge when he heard a noise just behind him. He turned and saw a big man pointing a gun at him, and coming toward him. The man came closer. Now George could see his face. It was Henry!

George had never met a runaway servant before. Now he knew they were dangerous—one look at Henry was enough. His eyes glittered and his hands were trembling. He held a gun, too, with those trembling hands.

George knew his life was in danger but he didn't lose his head. "Put down your gun, Henry," he said quietly. "I'm your friend. I'm not going to tell anyone I saw you."

But Henry didn't lower his gun. "Drop your pistol right there on the ground," he ordered.

George dropped his pistol at once.

"Get into the barge. We're going to the island."

"All right. Jump in." George pushed off from the shore and turned the boat toward the island.

"If we meet a boat, don't you dare to holler!" said Henry. "Don't you dare!"

"Of course not. You're holding the gun."

"Nothing can stop me!" said Henry savagely. "Nothing and nobody."

"I'll have to be careful," George thought. "He's not himself; he's likely to do anything. Maybe I can talk him out of being afraid of me. I'll have to or I won't live to get to the island."

152

"Henry," said George gently, "if you want to run away, that's your business. My father wouldn't even hunt for a runaway servant. My mother won't either."

"Your uncle does. He gets the bloodhounds out."

George went on as if he hadn't heard. "My father used to say that runaways aren't worth their salt if you have to bring them back."

"They're thinking all the time about being free. That's how I am. Can't think about anything else."

"How can you make a living if you do get away?"

"I have friends. You needn't try to talk me out of it. I'm going to be free, I tell you! I'm going to be free if I have to die for it!"

Henry was getting excited again. And those shaking hands still held a gun!

George knew his danger but he went on talking calmly. "Why didn't you just take the barge?"

"I was going to, but had to wait till dark to get away. Didn't plan to meet up with you."

"The island is the first place they will look for you."

"They will tomorrow. But I won't be there."

"What's the use of going there now?"

"Because of you. I'm going to leave you there. You're not going to send any dogs after me."

"I wouldn't do that!" cried George. "Why, you've been good to me since I was a little boy."

"How do I know you won't?"

"Because I say so. Don't you believe me?"

"I won't believe any one. I'm just fixing it so you can't do anything."

George was sure now that Henry meant to kill him on the island. He'd have to do something quick—they were almost there. But what could he do? He had no weapon.

Suddenly a thought flashed into his mind. He'd pole the barge end-up on a rock! He was close to a boulder now. He prayed that Henry wouldn't notice what he was doing.

Henry didn't notice. Suddenly, there was a great bump! The barge hit a rock, and Henry was thrown down. He dropped his gun.

George sprang for it. Henry grabbed at him, but missed. And before he could get on his feet, George was pointing the gun at him.

"What are you going to do with me?" Henry asked.

"What were you going to do with me?" George asked.

"Just tie you up to a tree and leave you. I figured Rastus would find you, come daylight."

"Well, I'm going to leave you here, too, but I won't tie you up."

"You're not going to take me back?"

"No. I said it was your business if you wanted

to go. You wouldn't be any account to my uncle if you stayed."

"God bless you, Mister George! I hope this won't get you into trouble. They can put you in jail for helping me."

"I can't keep you from jumping overboard, Henry. And I couldn't follow you in the dark."

"God bless you!" the big servant said again. Then in another minute he had jumped overboard and was swimming away in the dark.

George poled his barge off the rock and went home.

Mr. Willis sent men to hunt for Henry, but they couldn't find a trace of him. It made a lot of talk but none of it came from George Washington—not one word.

One in a Million

THE four new suits were having a chance at last. George was at his brother's beautiful home on the Potomac River, Mount Vernon.

He had been there since December, and now it was March first. But heavy rains had flooded the low lands. It had been impossible to survey them.

However, rain didn't keep company away. The house was always full of guests who stayed a week or a month, or as long as they wished.

Of course the strong young surveyor wasn't afraid of rain. But he had to wait for the swamps to dry up.

So he was at Mount Vernon for his sixteenth birthday, February the twenty-second. There was a big birthday party for him, and relatives came from far and near. His mother came with Betty and Sam. Austin came with his wife. The Willis family came from Fredericksburg. The neighbors came with their children.

George wore his light blue satin suit—the coat lined with white satin. His hair was powdered white and tied with a black ribbon. His low shoes were black and had silver buckles. He looked very grand and very, very handsome.

Almost everyone spoke of it to Mary Washington. But she wouldn't say George was handsome. No indeed! It might spoil him.

"George is a good boy," she said. And that's all she would say.

The older guests spoke about George's beautiful manners. "He always does the right thing," they said.

"No one ever saw George keep the best seat by the fire," said one.

"Nor does he sit when others stand," said another.

"Nor talk when others speak," said still another.

On Sundays everyone went to church. Then George wore his dark blue velvet suit. He sat tall and straight in the Washington pew. He scarcely moved till the sermon was over. He never forgot good manners.

He wore his dark plum-color cloth suit every day and for quiet evenings in the music room. George loved to listen to some guest playing the harpsichord. Sometimes he would slip in there alone and play it himself. He liked the harp-like tones.

At last the rain stopped. The sun shone warm and the swamps dried up. George surveyed every day, in his Indian buckskin suit.

A Negro helper carried the chain and drove the stakes. And with no other help at all, George measured the big plantation. He was very careful with his figures and maps. He made them exactly right.

Lawrence was delighted. "Now at last I know where my land begins and ends," he said. He wanted to pay George for his work, but the boy wouldn't take a penny.

"It will pay for my suits," he said.

"But I gave them to you, George."

"That's too much of a present, Lawrence. Besides, Mother would be angry if I took money from you."

That settled it. What Mary Washington said settled everything with those two good sons.

Mr. Lawrence Washington was so proud of his brother's survey, he showed it to everyone—guests, neighbors, and relatives.

"It looks like the work of an old surveyor," said a man.

"You wouldn't dream it was made by a boy of sixteen," said another.

"It will be good a hundred years from now," said another.

"I'd like him to survey my land," said the fourth man.

This man, Lord Fairfax, was an Englishman, but he had come to Virginia to live. He owned a large tract beyond the Allegheny Mountains. It was wild land and had not been surveyed.

Presently Lord Fairfax was at Mount Vernon talking to George. "My cousin, William Fairfax, is going out to survey my land," he said. "Of course, he can't measure such a large tract without help. I hoped I could persuade you to assist him."

"I should like to very much, your lordship. It would be an honor to work under Mr. Fairfax." George Washington knew how to be polite.

"There will also be another surveyor—Mr. James Genn. He understands the Indian language. That I think very important. You might have trouble with Indians."

"I'll be pleased to work with Mr. Genn, sir."

"You'll be gone a month or more, and it will be a long, hard journey. There will be no soft beds, my boy. Probably no beds at all."

"I understand that, sir."

"You'll have to do your own cooking and wash your own clothes. You'll be eaten up by mosquitoes. You may have to drive wolves away from your camps."

"I've been through all that on long hunting trips," said George. "I don't mind hardships. The fact is, I like them. You've got to be looking out for yourself all the time. It's exciting. Of course I'll go. When do we start?"

"Ah, but wait until you know what I will pay. You are interested in that, aren't you?"

"Yes, sir! But I know that you'll pay whatever you think is fair. Why don't you wait until you've seen my work? Then you can pay me what you think it is worth."

"Well, then, it is settled. A week will be needed to pack your instruments and supplies. William has a tent for your sleeping quarters."

"That means at least three pack horses," said George.

"We counted on three. Can you be ready a week from today?"

"I will be ready, your lordship."

George was delighted. What an adventure! New lands! New trails! It was like setting out on an ocean. One never knew what would happen. He wished he were starting tomorrow.

THEN ONE MORNING——

A month had passed since the three surveyors left. Everyone was worried, but no one said anything. A man had to do his work. If it took him into the wilderness, then that was the way it had to be. There was no use to cry about it.

Then one morning, here they were! William Fairfax, James Genn, George Washington! They had had a long, hard trip, but they were alive. They had been soaked with rain and frozen with cold, but they were well. And they had done what they had been sent to do—they had surveyed his lordship's wilderness lands.

Lord Fairfax studied the surveys and said he was very pleased. He paid the three surveyors far more than they had hoped for.

Now George was going to Ferry Farm to see his family. He was proud of the money he had earned, and he wanted to tell them.

He knew what he would do with the money—he would buy land and raise crops. You didn't catch George Washington wasting his money on foolish things. But of course he'd get those presents first.

The morning George left, Lawrence talked with him alone. "George," he said gravely, "I want you to come back as soon as Mother can spare you. I've not been feeling so well lately. I need you to help me."

George looked at his brother quickly. He was thinner, and he was coughing more.

166

"I'll come back right away, Lawrence. Mother won't need me. Sam is taking my place, and the other boys help, too."

"I might want you to run Mount Vernon for a time. I may go away for my health."

"I don't know about running such a big plantation——"

"You can do it. You're a good farmer."

"That's what I'm going to be," said George. "I decided that while I was away."

"And give up surveying?"

"Oh, no, no indeed! But I saw such rich soil. It made me want to raise things. I think I'll be both a surveyor and a farmer."

CLEVER AND FEARLESS GEORGE

At this very time William Fairfax was telling his cousin about the trip: "We had some bad wind storms and bad luck," he said. "One night

167

our tent blew down. The next night our straw bed caught fire."

"That was bad," said Lord Fairfax. "Where did you sleep after that?"

"On the ground, unless it rained. Then, in some settler's cabin on the floor, along with the dogs and cats and fleas."

The older man smiled. "How did George like that?"

"He didn't complain about anything. He took whatever came—flooded streams, mud, cold, lice, ticks—it was all the same to him."

168

"That's the spirit of a soldier. George would make a good one."

"He would indeed!" said William. "He'd make a splendid officer. No matter what happened he didn't lose his head. And he had no fear of anything."

"Not even Indians?"

"Not even Indians," answered William. "We were suddenly surrounded by them one morning. There were at least thirty of them."

"Go on," said his lordship. "Go on."

"We were ready to break camp. Breakfast was over. We had our own horses saddled. And the pack horses were ready with their loads."

"Why didn't you just ride away?"

"You can't treat Indians like that if they want to talk. And these Indians did. They told Mr. Genn they had been making war on another tribe. They were angry because they had only one scalp."

169

"They might have decided to get yours!"

"We were afraid of that. We didn't know just what to do. Then George suddenly asked them to dance and gave them money."

"He shouldn't have done that—he should have got away—you all should."

"You don't understand, cousin. George planned the dance so we could get away."

"Ah, indeed!"

"You see, an Indian doesn't dance hit-and-miss, the way we do. He has many different steps and motions. And he must do these at exactly the same time as the other dancers. That takes thought."

"I can see that."

"He must keep his mind on his dancing. George knew that and counted on it. And it worked! I don't think they saw us leave."

"That was very clever," said his lordship.

"George was clever about everything," said William Fairfax. "Just look at his maps and figures. Have you ever seen better surveys?"

"No, William, I never have, not even in England. Did he do this work alone?"

"Every bit of it. I didn't even survey with him after the first week."

"It's a beautiful piece of work. George Washington is a boy in a thousand."

"He's one in a million, cousin."

A BOY BECOMES A MAN

George kept his promise to go to Mount Vernon to live. He helped Lawrence manage the plantation whenever he could, but he was often away on long surveying trips.

More and more people were going farther west to live. They needed someone to survey the land and make maps to show where each piece of property was located. George had proved that he was a good surveyor, so he was very busy.

Early in the fall of 1751, Lawrence decided to go far away to a warm, sunny island to spend the winter. He hoped that living in a warm, dry climate would be good for his health.

"George," he said one day, "I asked you once to stay at Mount Vernon if I went away for my health. Now I have decided to go. But instead of leaving you here, I'd like to have you go with me. Will you go?"

"I would enjoy going," said George. "I gave up the idea of being a sailor, but I always have wanted to take an ocean trip."

A few days later the brothers sailed away to a warm island. At first, they greatly enjoyed being there. The people invited them to parties and made them feel very much at home.

Then George caught smallpox and had to spend three weeks in bed. And Lawrence found that the climate was not helping him.

Before spring, both brothers were back in Virginia. Lawrence was no better, but he was happy to spend the last months of his life at home. He died in July. George, who was only twenty, became master of Mount Vernon.

George managed the plantation well. He also took part in everything that made the colony a better place in which to live.

He was an officer in the Virginia militia, a group of citizens who served as part-time soldiers. Most of the time these men stayed at home and earned a living for their families. In time of trouble, they went wherever they were needed to fight for the colony.

Although George was now spending most of his time as a soldier, he managed to return to Mount Vernon for short visits. On one of these visits he decided to make a trip to Williamsburg, the capital city of the colony.

Along the way, he stopped to visit at the home of some friends, the Chamberlynes. When he arrived, he found that they had another guest, a young widow whose name was Martha Custis.

174

It did not take George and Martha long to decide that they wanted to be married. They had a little trouble setting the date, because George had to go back to the war in the wilderness for a while. Soon the danger there seemed to be over, and he was able to come home to stay.

George and Martha were married early in

January, 1759. The wedding took place in Martha's plantation home. It was not a huge wedding, but it was a very beautiful one.

After the wedding, George and Martha went to Williamsburg. For several months they lived there while George served as a member of the Virginia legislature.

The people had elected George to the legislature because they trusted him. They thought he would be a good person to help make the laws for the colony.

George was a good lawmaker, but he was eager to return to Mount Vernon. Martha, too, was looking forward to her new life there.

They had hoped to start as soon as the meetings of the legislature ended in April. But the roads were so bad that they had to wait for a while. At last, in May, George took his wife home to Mount Vernon to live.

The First
President

MANY years had passed. One morning in April, 1789, the Washington coach set out from Mount Vernon. It was drawn by six fine black horses.

The coach was white, with cushions of scarlet velvet. The Negro coachman and footman wore scarlet and white uniforms.

In this elegant coach rode General George Washington. His hair was now a little gray. But he sat erect, just as he did when he was young.

Facing him, on the opposite seat, was his cousin and friend, Colonel Lewis Willis. He was also a little gray, but he also sat erect.

General Washington had just received the

greatest honor ever paid to any American. He had been elected President of the United States of America. He had been made the *first* President of this new nation.

The capital was New York City then, in 1789. So the President had to live there. He had also to be there by a certain time.

His wife, Martha Washington, would come later on. Her coach would be piled high with her luggage. There would be trunks filled with

178

beautiful dresses, velvet coats, satin slippers with
diamond buckles, lace fans, and jewels.

She would travel in the same white and scarlet
coach drawn by the six black horses. Her coachman would wear the scarlet and white uniform.
And Rastus would be his name.

The General had arranged that before he left.
"You can trust him, Martha," he had said. "If
the coach breaks down, Rastus will know what
to do. He's smart about things."

179

"He learned from you," Martha had said with a smile.

ON THE WAY

So President Washington traveled north with his cousin. And everywhere, in every village, town, and city, there were great crowds to cheer him.

They came on foot, on horseback , and in coaches. Everyone wanted to see this brave man who had been their hero for so long.

"He saved our country from the enemy!" cried a man.

"Aye!" cried another man. "He wanted no English king to rule America!"

"He made a country for us!" said a lawyer.

"But it took six years of fighting," said a tailor. "And not once in all that time did he see his own home."

180

"He wasn't the kind to give up," said a carpenter. "He didn't think of himself. He kept right on fighting till he had chased the British back into their ships."

"Aye!" exclaimed a preacher. "And happy was the day they left our land and sailed away to England."

"There never was a smarter commander," said a merchant. "He knew how to manage everything: his troops, supplies, repair shops, blacksmith shops, boat building—everything."

"He had managed such things for years on his great plantation at Mount Vernon," said a planter. "And directed many workmen besides."

"That's one reason he was made Commander-in-Chief," said an army officer. "Another reason was that he had been such a fine officer in the Indian wars."

"He was quite young in those wars," added an old lady. "He was only in his twenties."

"He is a wonderful leader," said an old Indian fighter. "I fought under him. The men would follow him anywhere."

"I could never understand why he became a soldier," said a woman. "He was a surveyor and was making money."

"He is also the richest planter in Virginia," said another woman. "He was only twenty when Lawrence died and left him Mount Vernon. His wife, Martha, is very wealthy, too."

"Then I am more puzzled than ever," said the first woman. "Why would he leave that lovely place for the hardships of a soldier's life?"

"I can tell you why," said the officer. "In the Indian wars he felt he must go to the aid of the poor settlers in the borderlands. He knew the wilderness better than anyone. So he thought it was his duty to go."

"It was the same thing in the War of the Revolution," said another officer. "He felt again that

182

it was his duty to fight. No one knew better the terrible hardships of war. But he loved his country so much he was willing to suffer them."

"Then he is a real patriot!" exclaimed the woman.

"There never was a greater one," replied the officer.

"He will make a great President," said a banker. "He is honest and careful. And he has never, in all his life, broken any promise to anyone."

"He is kind-hearted, too," said a preacher. "He is generous to the church and also to the poor."

"He has given money to our schools," said a Virginia schoolmaster.

"He has helped his younger brothers and their families," said an old lady. "None of them was as well off as George."

"He's always helping his mother, too," said an old gentleman. "He built a nice house for her in

Fredericksburg. She's living there now. She's a neighbor of mine."

"What does she think of her son's becoming President?" asked a doctor.

"Well," said the old gentleman, "we couldn't get much out of her. She only said, 'George was always a good boy.' "

THE ARRIVAL

The coach rolled on and on. It was late spring and the roads were good. Just outside Philadelphia, a company of soldiers met the President. They escorted him through the city with their flags waving and drums rolling. And all the way bells were ringing, cannon booming, people cheering.

At Trenton, New Jersey, the President was presented with a magnificent white horse. And here, in his honor, a great arch had been erected.

184

As he rode under it, a white-robed choir sang a song of welcome. Then little girls scattered flowers in his pathway.

Now he was near the end of the journey. There was only the ferry trip to New York City. That was made in a fine barge, trimmed in blue and red. The oarsmen wore white uniforms. Many other barges followed, filled with citizens come to welcome him. These barges also showed the red and white and blue.

The President's barge landed and he stepped ashore. Then bells rang, cannon roared, and the great crowd on the shore shouted and cheered.

People lifted up their children to see him. Others wept when they saw his face. Everyone was touched. He stood there before them, a splendid, noble man whose courage had never failed—a patriot, who had risked his life a thousand times in the service of his country.

They worshiped him. They would have knelt at his feet. To them he was indeed "The Father of His Country."

WASHINGTON, THE PRESIDENT

George Washington became President on April 30, 1789. At that time the country had only thirteen states, all east of the Appalachian Mountains. There were no states to the west.

At first, Washington was very busy getting

the new government started. He chose strong men to help him. He worked with Congress to get good laws passed for the country.

Early in his term of office, Washington visited all the states in the country. "Only by seeing how people live in these states can I be a good President," he said.

Washington visited first the states north of New York City. Later he made trips to the states south of New York City. Everywhere he went, the people welcomed him as a leader.

In 1790, Congress voted to move the government from New York City to Philadelphia. This city was to be the capital until another place farther south could be found.

Congress voted to locate the capital city somewhere along the Potomac River. Washington was to choose the exact place. He chose the spot where the city of Washington now stands.

Washington knew all that part of the country

well. The spot that he chose for the future capital was only a short distance up the Potomac River from Mount Vernon.

There was no city on the land that Washington chose, only open country. A city had to be built. There were no government buildings ready to use. These had to be built, too.

It took many years to build the new city and to put up the new government buildings. When the government buildings were ready to use, Washington was no longer President.

There was only one name for the new capital of the country. Everybody agreed that this city should be called Washington.

"We'll call it Washington," said one of the officials. "We'll give it the name of the man who has helped us more than anyone else to have a country of our own. Without him, we never would have had a United States of America."

Washington was President for eight years. He

worked hard to give his country a good start. All the while he was a wise leader.

When his time as President was nearly up, the people begged him to run for President again. He asked Martha what she thought of the matter.

"You have worked long and hard for your country," she said. "The time has come for you to let other good men take your place."

"That's right," George agreed. "Let's go back to Mount Vernon. Our house and our plantation are badly run down and need our care."

"Oh, good!" exclaimed Martha. "I've wanted to go back for a long time."

BACK TO MOUNT VERNON

In 1797 Washington and his wife, Martha, returned to Mount Vernon to live. Then within a few months they settled down to the quiet, everyday life on a plantation.

189

Usually the family had breakfast at about seven o'clock in the morning. Then Washington mounted his horse and rode about the plantation. He talked with the workers and told them what he wished them to do.

In the early afternoon he worked in his garden and enjoyed his beautiful flowers. Around the middle of the afternoon he stopped to have tea with Martha. From then on, until night, he wrote letters to his friends.

George and Martha saved the evening for their friends. Almost every evening they had guests for dinner. They entertained these guests at a long table in the dining room.

After dinner they took their guests to the large drawing room. Then everyone talked and told stories. Sometimes George told about his early days as a surveyor. Sometimes he told about things that had happened while he was a soldier or while he was President.

Even though Washington was no longer President, people in the government still called on him for help. John Adams, who took his place as President, asked his advice on many important problems.

Many members of Congress made trips to Mount Vernon to talk with him. They wanted to find out what he thought about some of the laws they had in mind.

"He is no longer President," they said, "but he still is our leader. More than anyone else, he knows what is best for our country."

Thus Washington lived on in the hearts of his countrymen. And he has lived on in the hearts of his countrymen ever since.